The number of people making claims to an Employment Tribunal is rising - with **100,000** cases in 2000.

But ACAS's free and impartial conciliation service continues to save everyone the time, money and unwanted publicity involved in a tribunal hearing.

In 2000, **71** % of complaints to Employment Tribunals result in settlement or withdrawal.

Whether your complaint is about being bullied at work, unfairly dismissed or discriminated against, ACAS has the experience to help.

your rights at work

a *TUC* guide

**KOGAN
PAGE**

First published in 2000

Reprinted 2002

Kogan Page Limited
120 Pentonville Road
London N1 9JN

British Library Cataloguing in Publication Data

A CIP record for this book is available from the British Library.

ISBN 0 7494 3364 7

Typeset by Kogan Page
Printed and bound in Great Britain by Thanet Press Ltd, Margate

Contents

Foreword

There can be few people at work today who don't enjoy a good moan about their job or their boss from time to time. It's all part of working life – something to talk about round the coffee machine or photocopier. Not many of these complaints are likely to involve employment law, at least not until we have a Standard of Workplace Beverages Act!

Despite a minority of really shocking workplaces, most employers are reasonably fair most of the time in Britain today. But even in the best managed workplaces things can go wrong. And big changes in people's lives, such as becoming a parent, can raise whole new problems at work. Jobs are more insecure. There are few that can now say that no one with a job like theirs has ever been made redundant. At times like this it can become very clear that the employment relationship is one-sided. Employers do hold most of the cards.

But not all. Everyone at work has some basic rights in law. You may well gain further protection from the contract you have with your employer. After nearly two decades of a government that celebrated macho-management and saw even basic rights at work as getting in the way of economic progress, there has been a whole new raft of rights at work introduced by the new government. Some, like the minimum wage and paid holiday rights, aim to protect workers from old-fashioned exploitation at the rough end of working life. Others try to address the new problems of the long-hours culture and the difficulties of getting a proper balance between life and work.

Everyone at work should therefore have a basic knowledge of employment law. This is what this book provides. Of course employment lawyers will have shelves of expert reference books, and if you take a case against your employer, you will need help. But many problems can be resolved long before they reach any formal stage. Simply knowing your rights will make you better able to argue an informal case. But after reading this book you should know whether it is worth seeking advice, and will better understand what you are told.

This is a book for everyone at work, both trade unionists and non-members. Not surprisingly, we know that union members do have the advantage of expert advice and extra channels to help them raise problems with employers. But we also know that many people are not union members. After reading this book you may conclude that joining a union is a vital piece of insurance against work-related problems, but our aim is not the hard sell and, wherever we can, we also give other sources of advice. Many local agencies can be extremely helpful, and there are a range of specialist services available by phone, which can help many.

We have done our best to make this book accurate at the time it was written, but inevitably we have had to simplify issues and new cases in the courts can change the way the law is applied quite radically. You cannot rely on the general advice provided by a book like this as a detailed guide to your own position. You should always take expert advice. In some chapters you will find some case studies. Although the names have been changed, and some of the arguments simplified, these are based on real cases, and give some idea of how the law deals with real life situations.

A team of TUC experts has written this book. Many have contributed to the process, but I would like to thank Sarah Veale, Nigel Stanley and Kay Carberry in particular who have played the biggest part in producing this valuable guide to your rights at work.

John Monks
General Secretary of the TUC

PATTINSON & BREWER
SOLICITORS

We have a proud record of advising trade unions and their members for more than a century. Our expertise covers the full range of employment, discrimination, personal injury, clinical negligence and trade union law, at both domestic and European Community level. We have been repeatedly recognised as a leading firm in both the Chambers and Legal 500 directories.

Partners of Pattinson & Brewer hold senior positions or are closely involved in The Institute of Employment Rights, The Association of Personal Injury Lawyers and a number of other bodies.

With offices in York, Bristol, Chatham and London, we aim to provide a friendly and accessible nationwide service.

To find out more about how we can help your union and its members visit our website at
www.pattinsonbrewer.co.uk
or contact our managing partner, John Davies, on
(020) 7400 5112.

Introduction

Your basic rights

Everyone at work is protected by a series of basic legal rights – some old and some new. Some protect you against the worst kinds of exploitation and unfair treatment. Some give you positive rights that provide some choice, and some voice, in your working life. And some are there to ensure your employer keeps his or her side of the basic bargain at the heart of any job – you work and in return you get paid and receive other benefits.

Most large employers are careful that their general employment practices stay within the law. If your employer is large enough to have a dedicated personnel or human resources section, then they should have the expertise that ensures they know their legal obligations. But that does not mean that everyone in the organization will always follow company policy.

And in any case there are still good and bad large employers. Many offer terms and conditions well in advance of the legal minimum. They know that treating their staff well and giving them a real say in the way that they do their work makes for a more productive workforce. Others, particularly those with many low paid jobs, may simply want to stay just on the right side of the law. These are the employers who describe the most modest advances in employee rights as red tape and burdens on business.

Many small firms are good employers. Small business organizations often say that their staff are treated like part of the family. This is no doubt true in the best organizations, even if not every family is always a picture of perfect happiness. But others are not good employers. Sometimes this is because they depend on poor wages and conditions for the success of their business. In Britain today there are still sweatshops that Dickens would recognize.

Many more get into difficulties simply because they do not know their legal obligations as employers, or do not know how to respond to a difficult situation. Even though Employment Tribunals do not expect them to have the same formal procedures as large firms, small businesses often end up losing cases because they simply do not have any procedures for resolving disputes or problems at work, or know how to set them up if needed.

Issues covered by the law

Even in the best run organizations things can go wrong. You can end up being bullied by your manager even though your employer has an anti-bullying policy. It may be that the behaviour of one of your colleagues is beginning to look like sexual harassment. Even in organizations with good health and safety records, you may be the unlucky one who does have a bad accident. Stress is on the increase everywhere.

Rapid economic change has led to many being made redundant in recent years. If you are young, skilled and live in the South East then this may be only a temporary setback to your career. For older employees it can be devastating. Many jobs have always been insecure, but fewer and fewer jobs can now be said to be secure for life.

You may be falsely accused of wrong doing, or a minor infringement of rules may be blown up into an excuse to dismiss you. You may be tempted to walk away, but you will still need a reference.

Becoming a parent probably puts more strain on your working life than anything else does. New rights to unpaid parental leave have been added to long established maternity provision.

Getting a proper balance between work and the rest of your life can be an issue for anyone. British workers work the longest hours in Europe. Some need the overtime. But many white-collar workers, who do not get overtime, are trapped in an increasingly US-style long-hours culture – where the first one home's a wimp and the number of hours you spend at your desk (whether you are working productively or not) is taken as a measure of your commitment.

Discrimination is still rife at work in Britain today. The Macpherson Report, conducted in the wake of Stephen Lawrence's murder, not only had some harsh things to say about the Metropolitan Police but established a new definition of institutional racism.

Men are still paid more than women. Disabled workers are now protected against discrimination, but face enormous difficulties getting a job.

All of these are issues where the law may be able to help you, or where you need to know what the law says. Everyone at work should have a basic knowledge of employment law.

What you might get from legal action

Not every employment dispute will, or should, end up in a court of law or require lawyers to get involved. Every so often you may read in the papers of a case where someone has won, if not quite a lottery-sized payout, then at least a substantial amount of money. But these cases are very much the exception. Awards are normally much smaller, and going to court, even the more informal Employment Tribunals that hear many work-related cases, can still be traumatic. If you need to buy your own legal advice, it can also be expensive.

This book is not, therefore, about how to win a jackpot at an Employment Tribunal – you have probably more chance with a lottery ticket. Nor do we advise that you should always go down the legal road to resolving problems at work. In most circumstances, except perhaps where you have lost your job, it should always be seen as a last resort.

But a simple knowledge of where you stand legally can often help resolve issues informally at an early stage. Simply dropping a hint that you are thinking of getting advice about early stages of RSI (Repetitive Strain Injury) can often be an effective way of getting a better chair and workstation. In general, letting your employer know that you have rights can often lead to a swift improvement, particularly if your employer is ignorant of the law.

Unions and employment rights

Resolving disputes is normally much easier in a company where unions are recognized. Nearly every basic recognition agreement between a union and an employer will have ways of resolving both individual and collective grievances. There will be proper procedures for dealing with disciplinary issues. This is sensible for both employers and employees. Companies, these days, are fond of asserting in their annual reports that their staff are their greatest asset. Ensuring they have ways of raising problems with a real expectation that they will be solved is one relatively modest way of demonstrating that in practice.

Reading some newspapers you might conclude that unions are quick to bring tribunal cases. In fact the opposite is true. Most tribunal cases come from non-union companies, particularly small employers. This is because they do not have the kind of procedures needed to ensure that disputes and grievances can be settled properly in-house or are ignorant of such basic employee rights as not being able to sack someone because they are pregnant.

How to raise an issue

It can be much more difficult to raise an issue in a non-union workplace. While you do have legal rights that can be enforced, it does not mean that this will be easy. The employment relationship is one-sided. If your employer wants to treat you badly because you have tried to raise a problem issue, then as long as they do it relatively subtly then they will probably get away with it. On the other hand it may be that your employer was completely unaware of the problem and is happy to deal with it informally. You must make your own judgement about how, or even whether, you raise an issue.

If you are not the only one with a grievance then there is strength in numbers. You and your colleagues should consider joining a union. There are new rights that allow union officers to represent you with your employer, even if they do not recognize a union, and if there is sufficient support then they must recognize and deal properly with your union (see Chapter 5).

Sometimes round robins or petitions have persuaded an employer that there is widespread dissatisfaction and they need to take action. In other cases an anonymous letter, which includes government publications, making it clear that the employer could be in legal difficulties, can bring about change. You might think about sending a delegation to your employer, with very clear backing from the rest of the workforce. Some issues – such as the Minimum Wage or health and safety issues – can be discussed with an outside body, and it can then raise problems with your employer without revealing who tipped it off in the first place.

If the worst comes to the worst you may be able to walk out of your job and claim what is known as 'constructive dismissal'. In other words you persuade an Employment Tribunal that your employer may not have formally sacked you, but they still forced you out of your job. However these claims are quite difficult to win and you should carefully read Chapter 7 and take further advice. And of course if you have already been sacked, then you may have nothing to lose by taking action.

Even if you take an action, and win it, it may still be an unpleasant and difficult experience. While many tribunal cases are over quickly, some can drag out or end up going through lengthy appeal stages. You may end up being cross-examined by an aggressive lawyer for your employer with the aim of showing you in the worst possible light. If it's a case with a media angle, this could be reported in the papers.

In general we think people should stand up for their rights. Bad employers do need tackling. A long and difficult case may end up clarifying the law, and thus help thousands of other people. But you should be aware of both the potential benefits *and* down sides of taking any action. You should always talk this through very carefully with an adviser before committing yourself to any course of action that could bring you into conflict with your employer.

As well as trade unions, there are many other advice agencies that may be able to help, such as your local Citizens Advice Bureau or law centre. There are a range of telephone help lines – some run by voluntary groups set up to deal with particular problems and others by official or publicly funded groups. The TUC has its own 'Know Your Rights Line' which can provide up-to-date leaflets on employment rights, and point you in the right direction if you want to know which union you should join. These are all listed at the end of the book.

Employment law

In a book like this, we can only provide a general introduction to employment law. Inevitably we have had to simplify many issues.

The law may even have changed since this book was written. As we will stress many times, you always need to take detailed advice about your particular circumstances. The rest of this chapter gives a basic introduction to your rights at work and explains some of the key concepts in employment law.

The first important thing to understand is the difference between an employee and a worker. In everyday conversation employee is probably just a slightly posh term for a worker, but in law they are quite different concepts. Employees have many more rights than workers. To understand the difference, you need to understand the nature of the contract between you and your employer, which we explain on page 8.

There are two different kinds of right. There is a basic floor of legal protection that every employee enjoys. In addition because there is a contract between you and your employer – you work and in return he or she pays you – most people have additional rights provided by this contract.

The law does not just protect you from a bad or unfair employer; it also imposes duties on you and allows your employer to take action against you if you are guilty of misconduct.

Statutory rights

The basic rights that provide a minimum floor for everyone derive from the law of the land and are known as statutory rights. These normally come either from a government initiative, like the Minimum Wage, or from Europe, like the working time directive.

Many of the new employment rights such as parental leave come from Europe, and are the result of negotiations between employers and unions at the European level. But the European directives that result from this process still need to be turned into UK law. This will normally be done through a set of legally binding regulations.

But while parliament makes new laws, the courts have to interpret them. Although laws are intended to be precise, they can never cover every eventuality. Inevitably they will contain words which are a matter of opinion, for example 'reasonable' is frequently found in employment law, and an employer's definition of reasonable may not be the same as an employee's he or she has just sacked.

Over time the courts will hear enough cases which require them to decide how to apply words like 'reasonable' for a body of what lawyers call 'case law' to develop. This makes it much easier to predict how a case will go when it gets to court, as normally the courts will want to make decisions in line with previous similar cases. Sometimes, however, a particular case will set an important new legal precedent, and will end up going through every possible appeal stage (see Chapter 8).

But much employment law is new, and there have not yet been many court cases. It is sometimes hard therefore to give precise guidance on how some new rights will be interpreted by the courts. And while the legal system is heavily based on case law, sometimes the courts can be persuaded to look again at an issue.

Another legal route sometimes used in employment law challenges whether the government has properly put European directives into UK law. European directives are often quite broadly drawn because they need to apply across the countries that make up the European Union, with all their different legal systems and industrial relations traditions. But while there is usually room for flexibility in some areas, sometimes a case will be brought using the argument that the UK government has not properly implemented a European directive.

Such cases can end up in the European Court of Justice – the European Union's court where European law is normally settled. An example of this process was the landmark case that found employers could not exclude part-time workers from company pension schemes. The court ruled that this was sex discrimination as part-time workers are more likely than full-time workers to be women.

Contractual rights

The second types of employment right you enjoy are called contractual rights, so termed because they flow from the contract between you and your employer. Your employment contract is a personal, legal agreement that governs your relationship with your employer.

Employment contracts are usually written down, and you will normally be given one before or when you start work. But even if you are not given a written contract, the courts will rule that a contract exists simply because you are being paid in return for working. Whether written or not, your contract will oblige your employer to pay you for work or services performed, to provide work for you, provide a safe working environment and behave in a 'reasonable' manner.

You are obliged to 'serve' (or to work or perform a service), to be 'obedient', to be competent and careful and act in good faith. These old-fashioned terms are still used in the courts. They are called 'implied' terms, because they are not necessarily written into the contract but are assumed by the courts to exist in any relationship between an employer and an employee or worker.

If you have a written contract then it will also include other terms that regulate the relationship you have with your employer. It is likely to include how much you will be paid, what notice of dismissal your employer must give you, and your entitlement to holidays. Because they are written down, unlike the implied terms, they are called 'express' terms.

Although these express terms are in addition to your statutory rights, they do impact on your more general legal rights. This is because they define the kind of employment relationship you have with your employer. As the next section explains, there are different types of relationship between employer and employed and each carries different entitlements to statutory rights.

Worker or employee

Whether you are a worker or an employee depends upon the contractual relationship you have with your employer. Every year court cases hang on this distinction, and unfortunately there is no easy definition. As the courts cannot agree on a simple test, we can only provide a rough rule of thumb.

If your employer provides work for you on a regular basis, says when and where it is to be done, supplies the tools or other equipment and pays tax and National Insurance on your behalf then you are almost certainly an employee.

If, on the other hand, you decide when you will work, make your own sickness and holiday arrangements and pay your own tax and National Insurance you are probably a self-employed person contracted to provide a service to the employer. This means you are a worker, not an employee. To introduce some more legal jargon, the relationship you have with your employer is a 'contract for services' rather than a 'contract of employment'.

Sometimes your employer will pay your tax and National Insurance but only ask you to come to work when work is available, for example, on a seasonal basis. In this situation, it is likely that you are a 'casual' worker.

It may be that you are given a contract of employment that states that you will only be required to come in when work is available. When it is not, you will not be paid. Some days you will not work at all, although you have to be available to work if your employer calls you. This sort of contract is commonly called a 'zero hours contract'. In this situation, you are an employee, but with no right to work (or pay, except for when you work).

Most people will clearly fit into one of these categories, but if you do not and fall between them then it might not be possible to definitively say which you are without a court or tribunal case. This is clearly a major problem, as many statutory rights, for example, the right to redundancy pay, only apply to employees.

Many people are happy to be self-employed and some occupations by their nature – such as journalism – are likely to have a significant proportion of self-employed workers. But some unscrupulous employers deliberately try and prevent the people who work for them becoming employees so that they do not enjoy proper employment protection. The government has taken powers to regulate this in the Employment Relations Act 1999, but it is unclear at the time of writing how widely this power will be used.

A further confusion is that the Inland Revenue uses its own stricter definitions to guard against bogus self-employment being used as a tax dodge. It is perfectly possible therefore to be taxed as an employee, but to be legally self-employed. You cannot therefore use your tax status as a guide to your employment status. There is an obvious degree of unfairness here. The law allows an employer to get away with denying you employment rights, but still makes sure you do not get the more favourable tax treatment enjoyed by the self-employed.

If the law ever gets involved in defining your employment status then the courts will look at all relevant factors. Remember that your own views on whether or not you are self-employed may not be the same as those of your employer, or of the courts.

As we said at the start of this section there are a lot of grey areas here. Take for example someone who works as a cleaner in private households, working every Monday for one family, every Tuesday for another and so on. If you are in this position it is possible to be either self-employed or an employee of each family for whom you work. If you are paid by the hour, work set hours and only use cleaning tools provided by each family then you are probably employed.

If the working arrangement is more flexible then you may very well be self-employed. Say you clean the house and go when you've finished, with some choice about when you do it, with no set hours, use your own tools and are free to send a friend instead. It is pretty clear here that you are being paid to perform a service, rather than being given a job. You are still a worker, but you are not an employee.

So, if you are an employee you have a 'contract of employment' with your employer. Normally this will be written down, but if it is not then the courts will still consider that a contract exists between you and your employer. If necessary they will rule on your contractual rights by looking at what your employer may have said to you, the custom and practice established since your employment began and anything else that can help them establish the contractual relationship between you and your employer.

If you are an employee you will also enjoy the statutory rights described throughout this book, although many only start after you have worked for your employer for a qualifying period, for example, one year for protection against unfair dismissal.

If you are a worker, but not an employee, then you do not have a contract of employment. It is likely that instead you have 'a contract for services'. You still enjoy some statutory rights, for example, the Minimum Wage, but you will miss out on many others. There is more about your contract in the next chapter.

1 *Starting a job*

The law starts to protect you as soon as you apply for a job. When you start work you gain more protection, and other rights kick in the longer you work for your employer.

Applying for and getting a job

You have some rights as soon as you apply for a job. When drawing up a shortlist or appointing the successful candidate, your employer must not discriminate against you because of your sex, race or disability. Nor can an employer rule you out because you are a member of a trade union or have a record of activity as a trade union member.

Employers can, however, legally discriminate against you on other grounds such as your age or because you are gay or lesbian. The government disapproves of such discrimination – and there is a code of practice on age discrimination which good employers will follow – but you do not have legal protection. Chapter 6 covers discrimination law in more detail.

At some stage during the appointments process, your prospective employer is likely to ask for a reference. This is normally a statement from your previous employer or from your school or college saying that in their opinion you would be able to do the job. If the reference turns out to be inaccurate it could, in some circumstances, provide your employer with grounds to dismiss you. There have also been cases where employers have challenged reference providers and accused them of giving an over-favourable reference in order to get rid of someone.

Most application forms are clear that if you are found to have lied when filling in the form you will be liable to dismissal. In the past, few employers have bothered to check the facts on an application form but companies are now being established that will check CVs and application forms for dishonesty, such as 'exaggerating' educational qualifications. This must be done with your agreement, but in reality there is not much of a choice as you will be very unlikely to be considered for the job if you refuse. Honesty is, therefore, the best policy, but there are many ways of presenting your achievements in the best possible light and many books will provide tips.

As well as asking whether he or she can check your references with an agency, an employer may ask you to take a drugs test. Again you can refuse, but an employer can make that refusal the grounds for not giving you the job. This would only be illegal if he or she was treating different applicants in different ways based on their race or sex. If, for example, only black applicants with dreadlocks were being asked to take a drugs test, then this would be illegal racial discrimination.

Under the Immigration and Asylum Act 1996 your employer must ask you for your National Insurance number or some other evidence that you have a legal right to work in the UK. Employers must make this check for all new employees. If they limited it to one racial group or chose people they thought had a foreign name they would be guilty of racial discrimination.

Employers may ask you about any criminal convictions you have. But you do not have to reveal them if they are 'spent'. This means they happened long enough ago for the Rehabilitation of Offenders Act 1974 to allow you to keep them secret. For more information contact the National Association for the Care and Resettlement of Offenders (NACRO) whose contact details are included at the end of the book (page 160).

If your prospective employer wants to guarantee they know about anyone's criminal record or lack of one, from spring 2001, the Police Act 1997 allows them to ask you to provide a criminal conviction certificate. This is an official document that states whether or not you have an unspent criminal record. These will be available from spring 2001 and are likely to cost between £10 and £20.

Understandably, checks are tougher if you want to work with children. Your prospective employer must check with the police that you have no convictions involving children. If you are not working with children, you only need to tell your employer about unspent criminal convictions if you are asked.

When you accept a job offer

As soon as you have been offered a job and have accepted it, there is a basic legal contract between you and the employer, even if you have received nothing in writing. This works two ways. Firstly, it means that your employer has promised you a job. If the offer is withdrawn it may be possible to sue your prospective employer, particularly if you have suffered loss because you have left your previous job. Breaking a contract is known as a breach of contract in legal jargon. If a court decides that your contract has been breached, it can order your employer to pay you 'damages' or compensation. Secondly, it means that you have accepted the terms that are offered.

Contractual rights

You may not be given a document called 'a contract of employment'. Instead you might be given something called a staff handbook or a similar title. If you are, you may find some small print that says which sections are part of your contract of employment and therefore legally binding, and which bits are there simply for information. For example the disciplinary and holiday arrangements are likely to be part of your contract of employment, but the location of coffee machines in your workplace is not.

With one minor exception (redundancy payments for employees with a fixed term contract) your contract cannot remove or reduce your statutory rights. Even if you sign a contract in which you agree to receive less than the Minimum Wage or sign away your rights to claim unfair dismissal, you are still protected. If a case went to court, any clause that undercut your legal rights would be struck out as 'void'.

In the Introduction we looked at implied terms – those assumed by the court to be in any contract of employment; and express terms – those written down. But there are other ways you can gain contractual rights. If you work for an employer that recognizes a trade union and negotiates with the union about the terms and conditions enjoyed by you or people doing your job, then your contract can be changed as a result of an employer–union agreement. These changes apply whether or not you are a member of the union as long as the recognition agreement covers workers on your grade or doing your job. Normally, any change to a contract agreed as a result of union negotiations will be an improvement, but there will often be a trade-off involved – more time off and better pay for agreeing to work more flexible hours, for example.

The other way you can gain contractual rights is through what is called 'custom and practice'. This means that if your employer has done something for some time, for example, laundering staff uniforms, you would have a reasonable expectation that this would continue, and if it were to stop, you should be notified in advance.

All contracts work two ways, and your contract of employment can also put obligations on you. It may 'restrain' what you can do. For example, it might say you cannot work for a rival company for six months after leaving your current job. There may be confidentiality clauses that leave you open to legal action if you pass on sensitive information to others, although a new law provides protection for whistle-blowers (see pages 24–25) so if you tell commercial secrets to a rival then you could end up in court, but if you tell a watchdog about a pollution cover-up, then you will be safe if you have followed the right procedures.

Frustrated

Kevin Evans had been employed as one of two night service fitters. In April 1974, Kevin contracted industrial dermatitis and was off sick. He periodically sent in sickness certificates. In August 1974, the employer took on a replacement, but Kevin was not formally dismissed. In January 1976, Kevin recovered and turned up for work. But his boss told him there was no work for him, and gave him his P45. Kevin claimed unfair dismissal.

But Kevin lost. The tribunal ruled that his contract of employment had come to an end by frustration. This is a somewhat obscure legal term, but can crop up in contract of employment cases. Frustration occurs when some 'reasonably unforeseeable event' takes place that makes the contract impossible or unlawful to perform, or radically different from what the parties originally intended. It means the contract is no longer in operation. And as there is now no contract of employment, there is no job from which you can be dismissed.

Because frustration means there is no possibility of unfair dismissal employers have sometimes found it an attractive argument to use in tribunal cases. Tribunals have recognized that a finding of frustration of contract removes the right to claim unfair dismissal, and have therefore tended to impose a high onus of proof on employers who claim a contract of employment has been frustrated. The matters a tribunal would take into account in deciding that a contract has been frustrated include:

▌ length of previous employment;
▌ expected future duration of employment;
▌ nature of the job;
▌ employer's need for the job to be done and the need for a replacement to do it;
▌ the risk to the employer of acquiring employment protection obligations towards a replacement employee;
▌ whether an employee has continued to be paid;
▌ the acts and statements of the employer in relation to the employment (in other words, is there any evidence that the employer has acted as if the contract is still in existence);
▌ whether a reasonable employer could be expected to wait any longer for the employee to return.

It is important to note that there is no set time after which a contract is frustrated, and contracts have been found to run for nearly two years even though the employee had not done any work.

Your contract may also set out benefits other than your pay, such as details of your pension or company car. It may set out your grading system and provide information on increments, performance review, performance-related pay and promotion. In general if you work for a large company you are likely to get a detailed contract of employment that will cover most of the issues likely to arise between an employer and employee. If you work for a smaller company you may have a much more limited contract, even if you have a generally fair employer.

Both you and your employer are legally bound by the terms of your contract and by statutory laws. If you think your employer has broken the terms of your contract or broken a statutory law, you may be able to pursue a claim. There is a section on dealing with disputes about your contract in Chapter 5.

If you break the terms of your contract, this may be treated as a disciplinary matter by your employer or in extreme circumstances, could allow him or her to sue you, almost certainly after dismissing you as well. Of course if you have already left your job then a court case is the only option open to your former employer.

Contracts can be written in a way that allows your employer to make changes in your conditions. For example, your contract may state that you would normally work Mondays to Fridays but there may be times when you will be required to work on a Saturday. If your employer wants to change the terms of your contract, he or she should give you a statement setting out the new conditions and asking you to accept them.

If you do not agree, and do not in practice accept them, and your employer ignores this, then he or she is likely to be in breach of contract. This means that if the change is fundamental – such as changing your retirement age or cutting your wages – you can sue in the civil courts. If the court finds in your favour, it can order your employer to restore the original terms of your contract. But you will not succeed if the change is minor (see Chapter 6 for more on this).

Your 'written statement of employment particulars'

No later than two months after you have started your new job, you are entitled to a 'written statement of employment particulars'. This is a statement setting out your basic employment conditions. The written statement must include:

▌ your name and the name of your employer;

▌ the date when your employment started;

▌ your rate of pay (which must be at least at the rate of the National Minimum Wage), when you will be paid and how your pay has been calculated;

▌ your hours of work and your holiday entitlement, including public holidays (both of these must provide the maximum/minimum given under the Working Time Regulations);

▌ the title or description of your job and your place of work (this can state that you may be required to work in different locations);

▌ your notice period.

You must also be informed in the statement whether your employment is permanent or for a fixed term. A fixed term contract will specify when your employment will cease but your employer must still give you the required notice before your leaving date.

If you have signed a fixed term contract which lasts for at least two years you may be asked to waive your right to claim statutory redundancy pay (this is the only statutory right you can sign away – see also Chapter 8). You are *not* obliged to do this in law, but in practice your employer can make this a condition of getting the job.

You should also be given details of any agreement with a union about your terms and conditions (see above) and details of any requirement to work outside the UK. The statement can refer to other documents that you may have been given, for example, a staff handbook, which includes information about things such as your pension (if there is one). You must also be given information about your employer's grievance and disciplinary procedures (see also Chapter 5) unless your employer employs fewer than 20 employees, in which case the employer simply needs to tell you who to see with any grievance.

If you have already been given a contract of employment that covers everything that is required to be in your written statement, it will count as your written statement. Strictly speaking, your written statement is not a contract of employment but it can be used as evidence of your pay and conditions in any legal proceedings or for social security purposes.

You are also entitled to a written statement about your pay with, or before, your first wage packet or pay cheque. This is known as an 'itemized pay statement' (see Chapter 2 for more details of what this should include).

Other rights at work

There are many other rights at work. Some start on your first day of employment, others only after you have been in your job some time. The rest of this chapter lists the most important ones. Some only apply in practice to a small number of people or deal with very specific situations. We will mention them here, but you will need to go elsewhere for more detailed advice. Rights that everyone at work needs to know about are listed here and dealt with in more detail in later chapters. The chapter concludes with a list of rights and how long you have to wait before you are entitled to them.

Time off for public and workforce duties

All employees are entitled to reasonable unpaid time off to perform various public duties, including serving as a magistrate or a local authority councillor. Your contract of employment may give you a right to paid time off for such duties. Trade union representatives (where unions are recgonized), company pension fund trustees and designated health and safety representatives are also entitled to paid time off work to fulfil their duties.

Losing or leaving your job

Both you and your employer are entitled to a minimum period of notice of termination of employment. After one month's employment, you must give your employer at least one week's notice. Your employer must give you at least one week's notice for every year you have worked for him or her up to a maximum of 12 weeks, unless you are guilty of gross misconduct (for more about this see Chapter 5).

Once you have had your job for at least a year, you can ask for a written statement of reasons for your dismissal. You should be given one automatically if you get the sack while you are pregnant or on maternity leave, even if you have only just started your job. You are protected against unfair dismissal after a year's service, and in some special circumstances as soon as you have started a job (see Chapter 7).

Public and bank holidays

Contrary to popular belief, you have no statutory right to be off work on public or bank holidays. Your contract may give you that right, however. If it does and you are required to work on a public holiday, you may have something in your contract that provides for extra pay or time off in lieu. Your employer may count time off on public or bank holidays as part of your holiday entitlement. It is legal for such days off to count towards your statutory four weeks' annual leave under the Working Time Regulations (see Chapter 3).

Transfer of a business

If your company is taken over by another one, or if you work for a public authority and your job is transferred to a private company, your terms and conditions of employment transfer automatically to the new company. In other words, whatever is provided for in your contract continues and you will be counted as having continuity of employment. So, for example, you do not have to work another year before you can claim unfair dismissal.

You have the right to object to your contract being transferred to another company. But this can be dangerous. If you do object, but continue working for the new owner, the courts are likely to say that you have accepted the new contract. However if you do not object at the time of transfer but walk out once you have started because there has been a substantial change for the worse in your working conditions, then you may be able to claim constructive dismissal (see Chapter 7).

If you are dismissed by either your old or new employer simply because of the change in ownership then the dismissal is automatically unfair and you could claim at an Employment Tribunal. If, as is often unfortunately the case, takeovers and transfers do lead to job losses, then your employer must follow the procedures for redundancy in Chapter 7.

'Transfers of undertakings', as this area of employment law is known is particularly complex. European law, which has been recently revised, and UK law are both involved. If you have a problem in this area you will need good legal advice. A union or advice agency will be able to help.

Sunday working

Special protection has been introduced for some groups of workers when activities that were once prohibited on Sundays have been liberalized in recent years. These include shop workers and people who work in betting – either at racetracks or licensed betting offices. The aim was to allow people working in those sectors who did not want to work on Sundays to resist any employer pressure to start to do so.

You do not have this protection, however, if you have agreed a contract of employment that says you will work on Sundays. It is likely that staff taken on since the change of the law will have contracts that include Sunday working, but if you do not, or started work before the law changed, then you are protected. This means your employer cannot dismiss you, single you out for redundancy or punish you in any way for refusing to work on Sundays. You can get more information on this from your union or from the DTI (see addresses section in Chapter 9).

You only have special protection, however, if you work in one of these occupations. For everyone else Sunday is just another day of the week. Although in many jobs overtime payments or premiums are available for working on Sundays, there is no legal right to them.

Guarantee payments

If you are laid off for some reason, in other words, if there is no work for you on a particular day and you are sent home, you are entitled to a 'guarantee payment' for up to five days in any three month period. To get a guarantee payment, you must have worked for your employer for at least one month continuously, you must not have refused unreasonably to do other work offered by your employer, and the lay-off must not be because of a strike.

You do not have to be paid your contractual pay, unless your contract says that you will be paid if you are laid off, but you have to be paid the statutory minimum, which is currently £16.70 a day. If there is union recognition then better rates may well have been negotiated.

Insolvency of your employer

If your employer goes bust and cannot pay your wages, the state will make up at least some of your lost pay. You can claim what you have lost up to a maximum of £240 a week for up to eight weeks. As well as your basic wages you can claim any holiday pay, company pension or notice pay due to you. You must apply to what is known as the employer's representative, usually the liquidator or receiver. He or she will give you a form that you must complete and send to the address shown on the form. You will then receive payment.

Suspension on medical grounds

Your employer may suspend you from work for health and safety reasons when you are ill. This may be because your employer thinks you are be likely to do damage to yourself or your fellow employees if you worked. If this happens you are entitled to up to 26 weeks pay as long as you have worked for your employer continuously for one month and you make the claim within three months of the suspension starting. You must not refuse a reasonable offer of alternative work. The grounds for claiming medical suspension are strictly applied so you should get advice if you think this applies to you. You make your claim to an Employment Tribunal if your employer is not paying you, or you think he or she is not paying you the right amount.

Agency workers

All agency workers have some basic protection under the 1973 Employment Agencies Act. The government has recently improved this. If you are working for an employment agency you may or may not legally be an employee. At the very least you will be a worker, hired out to a company by the agency to perform a service. But the largest employment 'agencies' in the UK are not actually agencies in the strictest legal sense but businesses. They tend to employ their staff directly, as employees. Whether or not you are an employee, agency workers still have some basic rights. All agency workers:

▌ are covered by health and safety law, where the agency has a responsibility not to place you in a job for which you are not appropriately qualified and the hiring company is generally responsible for providing a healthy and safe working environment for you (see Chapter 5);

▌ are covered by discrimination law, which covers both the agency and the hiring company (see Chapter 6);

▌ are entitled to be paid the National Minimum Wage (see Chapter 2);

▌ are entitled not to work more than an average of 48 hours a week, unless you sign an agreement with the agency saying that you are willing to work longer hours (see Chapter 3);

▌ should receive four weeks' paid annual leave once you have worked for 13 weeks.

Some agencies have been getting round this by saying that your pay includes holiday pay and that they therefore do not have to pay extra if you take a break. Whether this is legal is not yet clear. It is always worth shopping around to see which agency will give you the best deal. If you are only looking for a short-term stop gap then holiday pay may not matter, but if you are looking to temp for some time or fear that you may not get a longer term job, then ask about holiday rights and pay.

As an agency worker you may also be entitled to Statutory Maternity Pay and Statutory Sick Pay, depending on your earnings and how long you have worked for the agency. You are allowed to join a union and some agencies encourage their workers to do so.

If you are working as an agency worker, and the hiring company offers you a permanent job, you are likely to be expected to work out a period of notice in the job as an agency temp before becoming a permanent employee of the company. Alternatively, the company may have to pay the agency a sum in lieu of notice. Any such arrangements have to be explained to you when you sign on with the agency.

There are other basic protections for agency workers:

▌ You have the right to be paid by your agency, on the agreed day, even if the hiring company has not paid the agency.

▌ You must be consulted before any changes are made to your contract or the terms under which you work.

▌ Different rules apply in the entertainment industry. For example it is legal to charge you a fee for trying to find you a job. If you are a musician, a performer, or work in some other capacity in the entertainment business through an agency, for example, as a camera operator, you should check what the rules are (see Chapter 9 for useful addresses).

Trade union rights

Everyone in the UK has the right to join a trade union. Joining a trade union is a private matter and you do not have to tell your employer that you have joined. On the other hand, you do not have to join a trade union and you have legal protection if you are discriminated against for not joining one.

You are free to join any union, or unions, which you choose. However, it makes sense to join a trade union that is already active in your workplace. If it has recognition rights with your employer then it will be in a strong position to look after you at work, accompany you if you have to go to a disciplinary hearing and so on. You will also have a say in any negotiations between the union and your employer.

But even if there is no union recognized, a union can still offer help and advice. Even if your employer says that he or she does not like unions and does not want you to join one, you can join without him or her finding out. Even if your employer finds out, he or she must not treat you differently as a result. It is illegal for an employer to discriminate on grounds of trade union membership or activity.

If there is a collective agreement with a union in your workplace, you may be entitled to time off for attending meetings organized by the union. You would also get time off for union duties if you volunteered to become a union representative in your workplace. For details about how to join a union, see Chapter 9, Further information, at the back of the book.

You are also protected against unfair dismissal for going on strike, as long as the strike is a legal one, that is, the union has held a ballot and met other legal conditions before calling you out. You are protected for the first eight weeks of the strike.

'Whistle-blowing'

Whistle-blowing is when you report to the authorities something seriously wrong or illegal taking place in the organization for which you work. You might find yourself in the situation where you find out that your employer, or someone in a position of responsibility in the organization, is guilty of theft, fraud or endangering staff, customers or the local community. There is new legal protection for whistle-blowers, but you need to have tried to raise the issue internally before going outside your employing organization to win protection. You can do this by using your workplace grievance procedure, or by going to a more senior manager, or a different manager to your own. If there is a union in your workplace, talk to it first. If this fails, you can go directly to the appropriate body, which may be the Health and Safety Executive, the Serious Fraud Office or the police.

If the employer dismisses you or punishes you for 'whistle-blowing', as long as you tried to raise the matter internally first, you will be able to claim reinstatement or compensation at an Employment Tribunal. The law providing for this is called the Public

Interest Disclosure Act 1998. Compensation for whistle-blowing is unlimited, although what you actually get would be calculated on the basis of your pay, length of service with the company, future employment prospects and so on.

You must have raised the matter internally first in order to be able to win a claim at a tribunal, unless it was genuinely impossible or impractical for you to do this, for example, if there was an immediate risk to somebody's life. Normally you would not be protected for telling the media. In that situation, you could also be at risk from a slander or libel action against you by your employer. This may well effectively gag you, even if you are in the right.

The Data Protection Act

The Data Protection Act 1998 gives you the right to know any information about you held by your employer. Your employer must also make sure that this is kept confidential. Only those with a legitimate reason to see data can do so, unless you have given your permission. Employers are not allowed to hold information about you that is not relevant to your employment with them. For example, it is not relevant for them to know that you are divorced. Nor are they allowed to maintain sensitive data on you, for example, relating to your sexuality, race, political or religious opinions or beliefs, union membership, health and criminal offences (except those covered under the Children Act 1989).

This law applies to data kept on electronic or paper files. The legislation allows you to see references from a previous employer relating to you, but not a reference provided by your current employer for a prospective new employer. If your employer will not tell you what data he or she is keeping on you, or passes information on to someone else without your permission, you may make a complaint to the Data Protection Registrar (see Chapter 9 for address).

The Human Rights Act

The new Human Rights Act gives you additional protection at work. It also gives you general rights as a citizen. As this law is new, and the rights it contains (drawn from the European Convention on Human Rights) are expressed in general terms, it is hard to know precisely how the courts will interpret it. However, the likely implications of the Act in the workplace flow from its rights to privacy, association and freedom of expression. If CCTV cameras are monitoring you, for example, and you object, you may have a privacy case. Interception of telephone calls made on the public network (but not calls on an internal system) is generally not allowed under the Interception of Communications Act 1985. This would not stop your employer from checking what calls you had made but he or she could not listen in on them.

The Human Rights Act further underpins the right to join a trade union and take part in trade union activities. It gives you the right of freedom of expression (subject to defamation laws and the provisions of the Race Relations Act). It also strengthens the right to a fair hearing in a court or tribunal.

Your rights timetable and how to use it

This is where we list all your most important statutory rights at work, how long you have to wait to be entitled to them (the qualifying period), how quickly you must make a formal application (the time limit) and the maximum compensation you can win (although actual awards are often much lower). The list starts with those that apply when you apply for a job and finishes with those for which you have to wait the longest.

Table 1.1   Your rights timetable

From when you apply for a job

Your complaint:	I've been discriminated against on grounds of race, sex, disability or trade union membership.		
Time period:	Three months.	*Maximum compensation:*	Unlimited.

More information in Chapter 6.

From your first day at work

Your complaint:	I've not been paid because my employer is insolvent or bankrupt.

Time period:	Three months from date on which bankruptcy declared.	*Maximum compensation*:	The smaller of £240 or a week's pay.

More information on page 21.

Your complaint:	There's been an unlawful deduction from my wages.

Time period:	None while in employment; within three months if employment terminates.	*Maximum compensation*:	The tribunal can order the employer to make up the difference, backdating it to when the deduction started.

More information on page 34.

Your complaint:	I have been dismissed or discriminated against because:
<ul><li>I've raised a health and safety problem.</li><li>I've become pregnant.</li><li>I'm a trade union member or pension-fund representative.</li><li>I've demanded to be paid the National Minimum Wage, insisted on my working time rights or taken other action against my employer.</li><li>I've taken reasonable time off for study or training, public duties or antenatal care.</li><li>I'm a shop worker or similar who has refused to work Sundays.</li><li>I blew the whistle on wrongdoing by my employer.</li><li>I complained about non-payment of Working Families Tax Credit.</li></ul>

| Time period: | Three months starting with date of (last) act or failure to act. | Maximum compensation: | Some of these rights have minimum compensation rates, eg, for health and safety dismissals the minimum is £3,300; some have maximum rates and others, for example, whistle-blowing, have no maximum. In some cases the tribunal can order the employer to make good, for example, to pay you the National Minimum Wage. |

More information on page 126.

Your complaint:	I've not been given an itemized pay statement.		
Time period:	None while in employment; within three months if employment terminates.	Maximum compensation:	The tribunal can order the employer to provide an itemized pay statement.

More information in Chapter 2.

Your complaint:	I'm not being paid the National Minimum Wage.		
Time period:	None while in employment, within three months after leaving a job	Maximum compensation:	The tribunal can order the employer to pay the difference between what you were paid and the National Minimum Wage.

More information on page 39.

Your complaint:	I've not been allowed to see the records I need to see to make sure I am getting the National Minimum Wage.		
Time period:	Three months after the fourteenth day following receipt of production notice unless a later date agreed.	Maximum compensation:	Tribunal can order access and/or compensation of up to £288.

More information on page 45.

Your complaint:	I've been dismissed because the owners of my business have changed.		
Time period:	Three months starting with the effective date of termination.	Maximum compensation:	Up to £240 per week's pay lost, to a limit of £4,880, plus up to £50,700 compensatory award.

More information on page 19.

Your complaint:	I've been dismissed or treated unfairly because I've 'asserted a statutory right', ie taken a case against my employer such as claiming unlawful deduction from wages.		
Time period:	Three months starting with date of dismissal or detriment.	Maximum compensation:	If dismissed, up to £240 per week's pay lost, to a limit of £4,880 plus up to £50,700 compensatory award. If still working, the tribunal can order compensation and order the employer to stop the unfair treatment. No maximum.

More information on page 120.

Your complaint:	My employer has breached my contract.

Time period:	Three months and only after termination at an employment tribunal; six years after the breach occurred in the courts.	*Maximum compensation*:	Maximum in tribunals of £25,000. Limit of £50,000 in lower (county or sheriff's courts), unlimited in higher courts.

More information on page 92.

Your complaint:	I've been sacked because of my sex, race or disability.

Time period:	Three months starting with effective date of termination.	*Maximum compensation*:	Unlimited.

More information in Chapter 6.

Your complaint:	I'm being denied 18 weeks' maternity leave.

Time period:	(not applicable).	*Maximum compensation*:	A week's pay for each week not allowed.

More information on page 65.

Your complaint:	I'm not getting the proper rest breaks set out in the working time rules.

Time period:	Three months starting on the day on which the failure occurred.	*Maximum compensation*:	Unlimited and/or the tribunal can order the employer to provide proper rest breaks for you.

More information on page 53.

Your complaint:	I'm getting paid less than people doing similar jobs because of my sex.		
Time period:	Six months starting with date of act complained of.	*Maximum compensation*:	Tribunal can order employer to provide equal pay and/or order compensation.

More information on page 106–09.

One month from the start of your job

Your complaint:	I've been laid off but not paid (guarantee pay).		
Time period:	Three months starting with day for which payment claimed.	*Maximum compensation*:	£16.70 per day.

More information on page 20.

Your complaint:	I have been suspended on medical grounds.		
Time period:	Three months starting with effective date of suspension.	*Maximum compensation*:	The pay you have lost.

More information on page 21.

Two months from the start of your job

Your complaint:	I've not been given a written statement of employment particulars.		
Time period:	None while in employment; within three months if employment terminates.	*Maximum compensation*:	The tribunal can order the employer to provide a written statement.

More information on page 16.

After 13 weeks employment

Your complaint:	I'm not getting paid holidays.		
Time period:	Three months from the date when the leave should have been permitted to begin.	*Maximum compensation:*	Unlimited and/or the tribunal can order the employer to give you your leave entitlement.

More information on page 50.

After a year in your job

Your complaint:	I've been dismissed unfairly.		
Time period:	Three calendar months from when you were dismissed.	*Maximum compensation:*	Up to £240 per week's pay lost, to a limit of £4,880, plus up to £51,700 compensatory award.

More information on page 120.

Your complaint:	I've not been given written reasons for dismissal.		
Time period:	Three months starting with effective date of termination.	*Maximum compensation:*	Two week's pay.

More information on page 118.

Your complaint:	I've not been allowed to return to work after additional maternity leave.		
Time period:	Three months after notified day of return when employer refuses right.	*Maximum compensation:*	Unlimited.

More information on page 68.

Your complaint:	I have not been allowed to take parental leave or time off for a family emergency under the terms of the regulations.		
Time period:	Three months.	*Maximum compensation*:	Unlimited.

More information on page 72.

After two years

Your complaint:	I've not been paid my redundancy pay.		
Time period:	Six months starting from the date of dismissal.	*Maximum compensation*:	See Chapter 7.

More information on page 130.

2 *Payday*

It is good to have a satisfying and worthwhile job, but most of us work because we need the money. This chapter sets out the law about your pay – what your employer must tell you, what he or she can deduct from your pay and the minimum he or she must pay you.

Deductions from wages

Your contract of employment or 'written statement of employment particulars' will say how much you are going to be paid. It must be at least the National Minimum Wage, described later in this chapter. If you do not receive the pay promised in your contract or written statement then your employer has made an 'unauthorized deduction from wages' and you can take a claim to an Employment Tribunal (see Chapter 8). This statutory right covers all workers, not just employees (see Introduction).

There are, however, three ways in which it is legal for your employer to take money from your wage or salary:

▌ Your employer can deduct income tax and National Insurance. This must be for the correct amount. If you think it is not, contact the Inland Revenue and it will repay you if the amount deducted was wrong, or investigate your employer if there is a suspicion of fraud.

▌ Your employer can take money if you have given permission. For example you may agree to make a payroll contribution to a charity, or to a staff social club or to a trade union. You can however withdraw your permission at any time.

▌ Your employer can make a deduction from your wage packet if your contract allows this to happen, as long as you have seen the contract with this in it before you start work, or your employer has explained in writing to you that he or she intends to take the money and you have agreed to it. This then becomes part of your contract.

If your employer has overpaid you the previous time you were paid, he or she may take that from your next pay packet without asking you. If your contract allows your employer to take money away as part of a disciplinary process, he or she can do this without asking you (see Chapter 5). If you take part in a strike your employer can take money from your wages without asking you. In this situation, your union will probably make a payment to you.

There are some jobs that allow your employer to deduct money if there is a cash shortage due to theft. The key test is whether you deal with the public and handle money. So if you are a shop worker, or your job involves selling goods to the public you can have money deducted from your wages if there is a shortfall. This can also happen if you collect money, say as a rent collector. But it does not apply if you only deal in business to business transactions, perhaps as a lorry driver supplying goods to a warehouse.

Your employer cannot deduct more than 10 per cent of your cheque, salary or wages packet. He or she can keep on making a 10 per cent deduction until the loss is paid off. The 10 per cent is before tax or National Insurance is deducted. Depending on your tax situation this may mean that in practice more or less than 10 per cent of your take home pay may be deducted. However, if you are leaving your job, whether because you have resigned, retired or been dismissed, your employer can deduct any amount of your final pay packet and any notice pay (see Chapter 7) to make up the shortfall.

Your employer must start making any deductions from your wages within 12 months of the loss occurring. But while he or she cannot start deductions after 12 months, they can continue if they have already started before the 12-month limit. A new deduction, however, would be unlawful and you can take a tribunal case.

The law on 'unauthorized deductions' covers issues such as holiday pay, bonuses, Statutory Sick Pay and luncheon vouchers. It does not cover loans or advances of wages, pensions or redundancy payments, tips, or payments in kind.

If you think that your employer has wrongly deducted money from your wages you should raise the matter with him or her first, or with the finance department if you work for a large company. It may be that a genuine mistake was made. If this is not the case, you can make a complaint to an Employment Tribunal (see Chapter 8) and they can order the employer to pay the money.

Sick pay rights

When they talk about their sick pay most workers mean the scheme operated by their employers. There are no national rules for these schemes, and many exclude some people, especially part-time and temporary workers.

But you do have rights to Statutory Sick Pay, a flat rate benefit, paid by your employer, in accordance with national rules. It is often called SSP for short. If you are covered, your employer must either pay you Statutory Sick Pay when you qualify; or open up the company scheme to you, and offer you benefits which are at least as good.

This is a complicated subject and this section has to simplify some points. If you have any problems claiming Statutory Sick Pay make sure you get advice and support from your union or an advice agency as soon as possible.

Qualifying for sick pay

You will qualify for Statutory Sick Pay if you:

▌ are an employee – see page 8 for the difference between an employee and a worker. As long as you are an employee it does not matter whether you work part-time or have only just started work with an employer;

▌ were over 16 and under 65 when your sickness began;

▌ earn enough to pay National Insurance Contributions (£67 a week till April 2001 when the limit is likely to rise a little).

You don't have to have actually paid any Contributions, earning above that level is enough to qualify. If your pay fluctuates, then entitlement depends on your average pay over the last 8 weeks.
   You will *not* qualify if you:

▌ are self-employed;

▌ have not started work yet;

▌ have a contract of employment that lasts less than three months – but people who have actually been employed for more than three months will usually qualify, even if their original contract was for less than that.

Claiming Statutory Sick Pay

▌ SSP is normally paid in the same way as your wages, and you claim it on a form from your employer.

▌ You can get it for up to 28 weeks if your sickness lasts that long.

▌ You will not be paid for the first three days – these are called 'waiting days'.

▌ Two periods of sickness within 56 days are treated as linked. This means that you won't face waiting days for the second. On the other hand, time off in the first will count towards the 28-week limit;

▌ You are not entitled to SSP once your contract of employment ends.

▌ Nor once your Maternity Allowance or Statutory Maternity Pay period begins, or, if you are not entitled to either of these for a pregnancy-related reason in the six weeks before your baby is due.

▌ Employers can ask for 'reasonable evidence' of incapacity. In practice, this means a self-certification form for the first seven days (including the waiting days) and a doctor's certificate after that.

▌ If your employer dismisses you to avoid paying SSP you may have a claim for unfair dismissal at an Employment Tribunal. The SSP rules, in any case, require her/him to go on paying you the SSP until you are no longer entitled to the benefit (or your contract comes to an end, if this is earlier).

▌ If there is a stoppage of work due to a trade dispute that began *before* you became sick you will not be entitled to SSP for the whole period of incapacity, even if the dispute ends. On the other hand, if the stoppage began *after* you became sick you will continue to be entitled to SSP.

How much will you get?

Statutory Sick Pay is paid at a flat rate of £60.20 a week. In April 2001 it is likely to be uprated by a little. Normally it is uprated each April. If you have two or more jobs, and earn more than enough to pay National Insurance Contributions in both, you can claim SSP in each.

Sick of the sack

Joyce Khan was a night-duty nurse, but became ill and was off sick for some time. Under NHS rules (part of her contract of employment) she was entitled to sick pay of two months' full pay and two months' half pay. But when this four-month period came to an end, Joyce was sacked.

However, the booklet setting out NHS sick pay provisions said nothing about dismissal at the end of the sick pay period. Her managers said that such a rule existed nationally in the Health Service and that it had been applied to other cases. But Joyce had, in fact, already sent in a medical certificate indicating that within 10 days of her sick pay running out she expected to be back on

---

duty. Apparently this certificate had never reached the attention of the officer who dealt with the dismissal.

She claimed unfair dismissal and won. The tribunal said that Joyce's managers had not acted reasonably. A rule that dismissal should be 'automatic' on termination of sick pay, regardless of individual circumstances, was outmoded. Secondly, there had been bad communication between departments concerning the medical certificate, and thirdly there had been no consultation with the employee concerned before dismissal.

Tribunal cases have established what an employer should do before dismissal for sickness, and there is guidance in the ACAS Code on Discipline. Employers should: consult the employee and discuss the problem with them; take steps to enable them to take a balanced view of the problem (this will include taking steps to ascertain the medical situation); consider whether suitable alternative work is available.

It is possible for an employer to fairly 'dismiss a worker for genuine sickness by reason of capability'. But tribunals tend to look carefully at the 'reasonableness' in such cases. They will consider: the length of past and future service of the employee; how vital the employee is to the employer's business, and how easy it is to find a temporary replacement; the effect of the absence on the business and other employees.

The question a tribunal will ask is whether the time has come where a reasonable employer is entitled to say 'enough is enough'. The key is then likely to be the future sickness of the worker. But the employer must also ensure that they are not breaking the Disability Discrimination Act (see Chapter 6).

The National Minimum Wage

The vast majority of workers and employees are entitled to the National Minimum Wage (or the NMW as we will call it in the rest of this chapter). You are covered whether or not you have a written contract of employment. Home workers, agency workers, agricultural workers and piece and commission workers are all entitled to the NMW. So are workers on temporary contracts and part-time workers. However 'casual' the work, you are still entitled to be paid the NMW.

The following groups are *not* entitled to the NMW:

▌ 16- and 17-year-olds;

▌ family workers, including those working for a family business.

▌ people working within a family, sharing tasks and leisure activities, for example au pairs;

▌ trainees on government-funded schemes, in particular, New Deal participants who are on either the Voluntary or Environmental Task Force options;

▌ apprentices aged 18 or aged 19 to 25 and in the first year of their apprenticeship;

▌ students on work placements, including teacher-training placements.

▌ the armed forces;

▌ prisoners;

▌ share fishermen;

▌ mariners and offshore workers if based entirely outside the UK;

▌ volunteers (who must work for a charity, voluntary organization, school or hospital and must not receive any payments other than reasonable expenses or benefits in kind or, in certain circumstances, subsistence payments).

The treatment of the self-employed can be complicated. As we saw in the Introduction it is possible to be a worker without being an employee. Both employees and workers are, however, covered by the NMW. If you have a contract for services rather than a contract of employment, then you are still entitled to the Minimum Wage. If however you are genuinely self-employed, effectively running your own business and cannot be said to have an employer then you are not covered by the NMW. Your tax status is once again not a guide to your Minimum Wage status. You can be treated as self-employed by the tax office, but still be eligible for the Minimum Wage. If in doubt, take advice.

National Minimum Wage hourly rates

You are entitled to be paid the NMW for each hour you work. But young workers are entitled to a lower rate than older workers, as are some workers receiving training. Hourly rates are currently:

adult workers aged 22 and over	£3.70
18 to 21 year olds	£3.20
training development rate	£3.20

Workers aged 22 and over receiving accredited training can be paid the training development rate in the first six months of starting a new job. After the initial six months, the worker must be paid the full adult rate even if the training is continuing.

Calculating your hourly pay

Hourly pay for the National Minimum Wage is worked out as an average over your pay period. If you are paid weekly, your pay period is a week. If you are paid daily it is a day, and if monthly, it is a month. Some people are paid in arrears. For example, your pay for the work you do one week may be actually paid in the next week. But you work out your Minimum Wage for the week the pay is earned, not the week it is paid.

Working out your hourly pay for most people is a simple matter of dividing your total pay (before tax and other deductions) by the number of hours you worked. But there can be complications, and there are rules both about what does and does not count as pay and how your hours of work are counted.

What counts as pay

Your pay may be made up of a mix of different elements. The following *do* count towards your hourly rate:

▌ gross pay – before national insurance, tax or pension deductions;

▌ piece rates, sales commissions, any performance-related pay;

▌ a bonus (though it must be allocated mainly to the pay period in which it is paid);

▌ tips paid through the payroll, though tips paid in cash directly to staff are in addition to your hourly rate.

The following do *not* count:

▌ pension, retirement or redundancy payments;

▌ overtime and shift payments;

▌ expenses or money spent on work refunded by the employer;

▌ allowances such as London Weighting;

▌ loans or advance of wages;

▌ any benefits in kind, such as meals, luncheon vouchers, car allowance or medical insurance, except accommodation which is dealt with below.

This means that any payments for overtime, for example, or London Weighting, must be in addition to an average hourly rate of at least the NMW. Your employer cannot pay you three pounds an hour for an eight hour day and then six pounds an hour for an extra four hours overtime, and claim that on average you were getting more than the Minimum Wage. Overtime payments cannot be used to boost a basic average which is below the NMW. Nor can an employer add a notional amount to your pay to take it to the Minimum Wage level but then deduct it again to pay for any meals or drinks provided free.

If accommodation is provided as part of your job, your employer can deduct a maximum of £2.85 for every day accommodation is provided or 50 pence an hour for every hour worked. This means that a maximum of £19.95 per week can be deducted for accommodation from your pay. If you work part-time, or the accommodation is not provided every day, the maximum amount that can be deducted will be less. If when you do your sums the hourly or daily allowances produce different answers, then it is the one that gives the smaller amount that is used.

What count as working hours

Hourly paid and salaried workers are entitled to be paid the NMW for time:

▌ at work and required to be at work;

▌ on standby or on-call at or near work;

▌ downtime at work caused by machine breakdown;

▌ travelling to business or training during normal working hours;

▌ training during normal working hours.

If you are hourly paid, the NMW legislation does not give you the right to be paid for rest breaks, sick leave or maternity leave. However, under your employment contract you may be entitled to be paid for these hours too.

Piece or commission workers

If you are a piece or commission worker you must still be paid at least the NMW on average for the hours worked. But as you are unlikely to have fixed hours, there are two ways of ensuring that you get the NMW. Either you can agree with your employer to become hourly paid or you can draw up a written 'fair estimate agreement' with your employer.

A fair estimate agreement sets out how long a particular task is likely to take. In order to protect you from being made to sign an agreement that is simply an excuse for not paying the NMW, the law rules out any agreement which estimates the time you will need to take to do a task at less than 80 per cent (or four-fifths) of the time it would take an average worker to do the same task.

In other words if you are a home worker stuffing envelopes, and are paid for every 100 you complete, you might agree with your employer that you can stuff 100 envelopes in 30 minutes. This is the fair estimate agreement. You must therefore be paid at least £1.85 for every 100 envelopes to ensure that you can earn £3.70 an hour. Of course if you can work more quickly you can earn extra. If you find that you are not earning the National Minimum Wage, then the fair estimate agreement is wrong. The law would support a challenge that the agreement was unfair if you could show an average worker could not do 100 envelopes in less than 37.5 minutes, as 30 is 80 per cent of 37.5.

A legal challenge in this situation may be difficult. The problem of course is that home workers are among the most vulnerable groups of workers, but action may still be possible. There are some contact details for advice on homework at the end of this book.

Unmeasured work

A small number of workers undertake 'unmeasured work'. This means they have fixed tasks, but no fixed hours of work. Examples might include hostel wardens or domestic workers with no fixed hours. Workers undertaking unmeasured work must either be paid at least the NMW for every hour worked, or can agree a 'daily average' agreement with their employer. This would identify the number of hours likely to be worked daily, and must be a realistic average. The worker must then be paid at least the NMW for this number of hours each day.

Your right to see your records

Employers are required to keep sufficient records to establish that they are paying workers at least the NMW and workers have the right to see and copy their records. If you want to see your records, you must ask your employer in writing. The employer must produce the records within 14 days. You have the right to be accompanied by someone of your choice when you inspect your records.

What to do if you are not receiving the NMW

Your rights

Under the NMW legislation, you have the right:

▌ to be paid at least NMW rates;

▌ to see your records (accompanied) as set out above;

▌ not to be dismissed or victimized as a result of attempts to be paid or ensure you are eligible for the NMW.

If you are not receiving the NMW, or have been refused access to your records or have been victimized as a result of trying to claim the NMW, you can get help to enforce your rights.

Take advice

If you are a trade union member, your union will be able to give you advice on your rights, accompany you to see your records and help you take a case to an employment tribunal if you are not receiving your rights. Other agencies including Low Pay Units around the country can also help and advise. Their numbers are given at the end of the book.

National helpline and enforcement officers

The Inland Revenue is responsible for enforcing the NMW. They run a national helpline, which gives information and advice on the NMW. Enforcement officers at the Inland Revenue can help you to work out whether you are receiving your rights, and take enforcement action against your employer if you are not. Calls are charged at local rates, and are confidential.

Enforcement officers have legal powers to enable them to enforce the NMW. They can require your employer to provide information about NMW pay, and inspect your employer's premises to gain access to pay records. If an enforcement officer believes that an employer is not paying the NMW, he or she can serve an enforcement notice that requires your employer to start paying you the NMW and pay you back pay.

If an employer ignores the enforcement notice, the enforcement officer can serve a penalty notice that levies fines of twice the NMW for each day since the enforcement notice was served for each worker who is owed money. These fines though, go to the government, not to you. The enforcement officers can also help workers take their employer to an employment tribunal, or take a case on behalf of the worker.

Deliberate refusal to pay the NMW is a criminal offence. If an employer continues to refuse payment, the enforcement officer can prosecute him or her in the criminal courts.

Employment tribunal or civil courts

You can take a case against your employer in an employment tribunal or in the civil courts to recover any money owed as a result of not receiving the NMW. It is up to the employer to show that he or she has paid you the NMW. You do not have to prove that you have not received it, though in practice you will need to be able to disprove your employer's claim.

You are, however, probably best advised to make every effort to get the Inland Revenue's enforcement officers to take up your case if possible, especially if it is a clear-cut case. Tribunals are more likely to hear test cases, where the rules are not entirely clear. For example sub-post office masters and mistresses have established that they are workers and therefore entitled to the NMW through tribunal cases.

If you have been refused access to your records, an employment tribunal can order your employer to pay you £288. You can also take a claim to an employment tribunal for unfair dismissal or victimization if you have lost your job or suffered some other action from your employer resulting from trying to get your right to be paid the NMW.

3 *Working time rights*

Thanks to Europe's working time directive, most people now have seven basic rights to proper time off, rest breaks and paid holiday:

▌ four weeks' paid holiday a year;

▌ a break when the working day is more than six hours;

▌ a rest period of 11 hours every working day;

▌ a rest period of 24 hours once every seven days;

▌ a ceiling of 48 hours on the maximum average working week;

▌ a ceiling of an average of eight hours' night work in every 24.

▌ free health assessment for night workers.

But working time rights are complicated, and have proved controversial. Employer organizations successfully lobbied our government for exemptions and opt-outs that do not apply in the rest of Europe. The European regulations, on which UK law is based, are far from comprehensive. Some groups are exempt, and there are many problems of definition such as what exactly counts as working time. Many provisions can be varied by agreement between the employer and the workforce.

We work longer hours than any other European country. In some industries and sectors this is because many hours of overtime are worked. Security guards working for the Minimum Wage need the overtime to earn a decent income. In other sectors long hours are built into the system, with junior hospital doctors probably the best-known example.

For white-collar workers the problem has got worse. The biggest growth in working hours in recent years has been among managers, professionals and those doing similar jobs. It is rare for employees doing these types of job to have their hours counted, as they will not normally get overtime. But many offices and other workplaces are gripped by a long-hours culture. Nothing is ever said directly but the sheer volume of work, pressure from colleagues, job insecurity and wanting to get on have all conspired to keep people at work for longer and longer hours.

Many such jobs are rewarding and interesting. Work does not always come along in neat nine to five parcels. But it is easy for working hours to ratchet up a little more each year. Work and family life get out of balance. Stress and exhaustion levels rise. To call time on Britain's long-hours culture is not to go back to clockwatching, but to understand that other countries manage to combine better living standards, shorter working hours and more productive workplaces.

Then of course there are those who are missing out on their most basic rights to paid holidays and proper rest breaks. When the Working Time Regulations first came into force in 1998, around 2 million people won their first ever rights to paid holidays. Some are still missing out, or are being made to pay in other ways for their own holidays.

This chapter aims to guide you through the working time maze. It cannot provide all the answers but it should tell you whether you are getting your working time rights, whether you are clearly missing out, or whether you are in a grey area where you will need to take detailed advice based on your own circumstances.

Exemptions from Working Time Regulations

Some groups of workers are completely exempt from all Working Time Regulations. Others miss out on some rights but not others. If you are under 18 the rules are different, and you should make sure you read the section on page 63 at the end of this chapter. The following groups are not covered (though some will be in the future):

▌ **Transport workers** – but not everyone who works for a transport company or in the transport sector counts as a transport worker. It does include anyone who actually travels. So if you are a driver or work on a bus or train then you do not have working time rights. Core transport staff such as ticket collectors also count, even though their workplace is fixed. But other staff who work at a transport location such as people who unload lorries or who work in shops in stations are covered by the working time rules.

▌ **Seafarers and offshore workers.**

▌ **Junior doctors in training.**

▌ **Armed forces and civil protection services** (such as the police) – but not all civil protection personnel are excluded. Ambulance personnel, fire-fighters and prison staff are covered by the regulations. You will need to take more advice if you work in this category. Most workers in civil protection outside the armed forces or the police are in a trade union. This should be your first port of call for further advice.

▌ **Domestic staff in a private household** are partially excluded. They are entitled to rest breaks and paid holidays, but not to the 48-hour average week or night work rights.

▌ **Those whose 'working time is not measured or pre-determined'** – although workers in this category are entitled to paid holidays, they are exempt from all other working time rights.

This last exemption has been the subject of much argument in Britain. The European regulations are clear that this is meant to be a narrow exclusion aimed at relatively small groups in the workforce. These include top managers who are free to set their own hours (perhaps because they own the business or have no one to tell them what to do), workers employed by other members of their family and some unusual jobs such as ministers of religion.

But employer organizations have argued that this exemption should apply to the majority of white-collar workers, for work they do on a 'voluntary' basis outside the hours set down in their contract of employment. Their lobbying persuaded the government to change the Working Time Regulations at the end of 1999. We explain this later in the chapter.

Happy holidays!

Everyone at work (apart from those in all but the last two exempt groups above) is now entitled to a minimum of four weeks' paid leave each year. The number of days you will actually receive as holiday depends on how many days a week you work. If you work full-time five days a week you should, therefore, get four lots of five days – that's 20 days – of paid leave every year.

If you work part-time you should get four times what you work on average each week. For example if you work three days a week then you should get (4x3=) 12 days' holiday.

But this is not in addition to bank holidays. Christmas Day and other holidays can count as part of your annual entitlement as long as you are paid for them. You can also take unpaid time off if you have young children or suffer a family emergency such as looking after a sick child. This is explained in Chapter 4.

When you can take your holidays

You do not have the right to choose when you take your holiday. This is almost entirely up to your employer. They can refuse requests, rule out all holiday at particular times of the year and even direct you to take your holiday when it suits them without any consultation with you. If you are requesting a holiday, the regulations say that you must give your employer sufficient notice. This is twice the number of days of leave that will be taken – to take four days off work you must therefore give eight working days' notice.

But while you must give this notice, it does not guarantee that you will get the holiday, as your employer is free to refuse leave requests. On the other hand there is nothing to stop your employer granting requests at extremely short notice for that matter. In practice most well-run organizations will have their own rules about deciding leave.

More importantly the same notice period applies to your employer if they are telling you when you must take a holiday. They cannot therefore force you to take a fortnight's leave because an order is suddenly cancelled. They must give you four weeks' notice – twice the period of the leave – if they are to make you take two weeks off.

Your employer must also give you notice if they want to rule out some periods when staff cannot take leave. The period of notice must be the same as the period during which holiday cannot be taken. In other words if the employer wants to stop people taking holidays for the four-week period before Christmas, then four weeks notice must be given.

Entitlement to holiday rights

You have to work for your employer for 13 weeks before you get holiday rights. Some less scrupulous employers are trying to get round holiday rights by giving their workers a series of 13-week contracts. A test case to discover whether this is legal has gone to the European Court, but is likely to take some time to be heard.

If you work for an agency, even if you move from placement to placement, then they must honour your holiday rights after 13 weeks continuous employment. Some try to do this by giving you extra pay each week which if you saved it over a year would pro-vide enough to provide your normal non-holiday pay for the time you are entitled to take off. It is unclear whether this is legal.

Holiday pay

If you work regular hours and get the same pay each week, then holiday pay is simply the same as your normal pay. If your normal pay includes regular bonuses or overtime payment then these should also be included in your holiday pay.

If your weekly pay varies, perhaps because you get different amounts of overtime each week, then your weekly holiday pay should be the average weekly pay you earned over the last 12 weeks. This should include overtime and any bonuses. Your employer should not reduce your holiday pay to your basic pay levels if you normally get overtime payments.

Holiday pay paid throughout the year

When paid holidays were first introduced in 1998, some people found a change to their pay slip. Their take home pay was still the same, but it was now made up of two elements. First was their basic pay, which had been reduced from what it had been in previous pay packets. The difference was made up with a second new element called holiday pay. The employer then said that there was no need for paid holidays as you were getting your holiday pay through the year and it was up to you to save it up.

This was almost certainly an illegal breach of the contract of employment, though if this happened to you, it is now too late to make a claim. If, however, you have agreed a contract that provides extra holiday pay in every pay packet instead of paid leave, then it is not yet clear whether this is within the law. A test case will probably revolve around whether this still allowed workers to have a holiday.

Changing jobs and holiday rights

You cannot take unused holiday from one job to another. When you leave a job you should get holiday pay for any unused holiday and may have to pay some holiday pay back if you have taken more holiday than you are entitled.

The amount is worked out using what is called your 'leave year'. This is the period during which you can take your four weeks' leave. Most workers will have a leave year defined as part of their contract of employment or in a staff handbook, and will be the same across the organization. If no leave year is defined in this way, then your leave year runs between each anniversary of when you started your job.

The amount of holiday you are entitled to for part of a leave year is worked out on an obvious basis. You get one-twelfth of your holiday entitlement for each month you have worked, which is one week's holiday for every three months of your leave year. If you leave after six months and have taken all your four weeks' leave then your employer could make you pay back two weeks' pay.

Days off and breaks

The basic rights are easily stated. You should get at least one day off every week and an uninterrupted break of 11 hours every day.

But it does not have to be the same day each week. As an example, your employer can meet the weekly rest requirement by giving you the first day of one week and the last day of the next. This means you can legally work 12 days in a row without a day off, as long as you then get two days off in a row.

If this were adopted as a regular work pattern it would mean you were getting two days off a fortnight, as the rest period on the last day of the second week would be followed by the rest day of the first week in the pattern.

But some workers and jobs are treated differently. These include:

▌ security guards, caretakers and other jobs where you need to be there to protect people and property;

▌ where the job involves long travelling distances;

▌ where the job requires continuity of service or production such as hospitals, prisons, docks, airports, media, post and telecommunications, civil protection (such as the police), agriculture, and industries where work cannot be interrupted (eg, utilities);

▌ jobs where there are seasonal rushes such as tourism, post and agriculture;

▌ shift workers when they are in the process of changing shift.

The right can also be suspended at any workplace for workers directly involved if there is an emergency or accident. However, if you fall into one of these categories, or are faced with an emergency, you do not lose the right to time off. Instead your employer must provide what the regulations call 'compensatory rest' (see below). This must provide the same time off, but at a time convenient to the employer.

Breaks at work

You are also entitled to a break of 20 minutes away from where you normally work if your working day is longer than six hours. But the same groups of workers, who have different provisions for daily and weekly breaks, can also have their breaks at work varied. Again if you cannot take your break you must be given 'compensatory rest' or time off at another time.

In some jobs you may be entitled to longer breaks for health and safety reasons. If your job is particularly repetitive or dangerous (keyboard workers liable to RSI are one example) then you may be entitled to more breaks. Take further advice if you are in this position. In a unionized workplace there will normally be a health and safety representative. If not, you can ask the Health and Safety Executive.

Agreeing provision

Provisions can be varied but only by agreement between the management and the relevant workforce collectively. Your boss cannot call you into his or her office and suggest that you give up or change your breaks, whether it is done politely or with threats of what might happen if you do not. Even through collective agreement you cannot agree to give up your entitlement to breaks, but their timing can be varied.

There are two main ways these agreements can be made. In the regulations these are called collective and workforce agreements. A collective agreement is made between recognized trade unions and management as part of the normal negotiating process. Typically some sensible flexibility will be agreed in return for some benefit. For example, a different break pattern might be agreed in return for longer breaks. Both sides can benefit from this type of agreement.

A workforce agreement can be made where there are no recognized unions. The employer will organize an election for workforce representatives who will then conclude an agreement. This is not a very satisfactory procedure. It is very much under the control of the employer. The representatives that are elected are unlikely to be experts on the working time regulations, have any training in how to negotiate or be able to call on expert outside advice. Without union back-up workforce representatives are much less likely to get a good deal.

If this is going on in your workplace, you may want to discuss with an appropriate union how best to use it as a way of unionizing your fellow workers. At the very least you should make sure the elected representatives are genuinely independent of the employer and are as briefed as they can be on what the regulations say.

Some minor provisions can also be varied in your contract of employment.

Working out 'compensatory rest'

Even if you fall into one of the categories, which means you are not covered by some of the rules on breaks, you should still get 'compensatory rest.' This means that you may have to take your breaks or time off at a different time. You can check this by working out how many hours a week in total you are getting as time off, either as breaks at work or between shifts. On average it should be more than 90 hours.

The rules for compensatory rest are not set out in detail, but the government suggests that you should not have to wait more than a couple of weeks for daily rest or more than a couple of months for weekly rest. If you look at your last eight weeks at work and find that you have not had 90 hours' average rest then your employer should be clear about how you can catch up.

The 48-hour working week

The basic right is easily stated – there should be a limit of 48 hours on the maximum average working week. But:

▌ some jobs are not covered at all (see the start of this chapter for a list of exempt groups);

▌ the 48-hour limit is an average – not a limit each week;

▌ the average is calculated in different ways for different types of job;

▌ individuals and groups of workers can change the way the limit applies or opt out from it altogether.

There are also some real problems defining some of the terms used in the regulations. Many modern (and some older) jobs have grey areas where there is room for argument about whether or not you are actually working. Some of these will probably need to be tested in the courts.

Defining working time

The basic definition of working time is that you need to be at your workplace and carrying out your working duties under the direction of your employer for it to count as working time. This means that it *does not include*:

▌ breaks;

▌ travel to work time;

▌ time when you are on call but not working;

▌ training at a college;

▌ time taken to travel to an occasional meeting away from your normal workplace.

It *does include*:

▌ overtime;

▌ training at the workplace provided by your employer;

▌ time taken travelling to visit clients when this is a regular part of your job such as a travelling salesman or home help;

▌ a working lunch.

The main arguments about the 48-hour average limit have been about how to define working time for white-collar workers. The regulations have been changed as a result and the government has also issued new guidance. The change to the regulations introduces a new type of working time for white-collar workers called 'partially unmeasured working time'. This applies for work that you choose to do in addition to the hours set out in your contract of employment. This was introduced because employers complained that some white-collar activities – such as taking material home to read over the weekend on a completely voluntary basis – could end up counting against the 48-hour average limit.

There are two tests that determine whether additional voluntary work counts as 'partially unmeasured working time'. First, it must be your genuine choice to do the extra work. Secondly, there must be an absence of what lawyers call detriment – in other words there would be no adverse consequences for you if you did not do the additional work.

The problem with this change is that there is a very fine line between some of the distinctions used. It is rare that white-collar workers are told, 'you will stay in the office until 7pm'. It is more likely to be the pressure of work and peer group pressure that leads to people working long hours. Employers are likely to claim that all white-collar work outside the hours set in the contract of employment is voluntary.

No one knows how the courts will interpret these provisions until there have been some test cases. You will need expert advice to pursue any kind of case on these grounds.

Working out your average limit

Some press reporting has suggested that the 48-hour limit applies every week. Except for the special case of night workers involved in dangerous work, this is incorrect. It is always an average limit. So even if you work more than 48 hours one week, if you work fewer the next then you may well have worked less than the 48-hour limit on average.

For most people you calculate your average by looking at your working time over the last 17 weeks. The period over which the average working time is measured is known in the regulations as the 'reference period'. To calculate this you need to add up your total working time for each of the last 17 weeks and then divide by 17.

If you were sick or took leave on any days during this period, you should start counting your reference period a week earlier. You should then include enough extra days from the week after the reference period to make up for days that you did not work during the 17 weeks. If there are not enough extra days then you keep starting the reference period earlier until you have enough to get a full 17-week reference period.

There are some exceptions to the 17-week reference period. In some jobs the time over which the average is worked out is extended to 26 weeks. These are the same groups as shown on page 53, who have reduced rights to choose when they take rest breaks. As with rest break rights, employers can switch to a 26-week reference period when there is an emergency.

If you have not yet worked for 17 weeks then you calculate the average from when you started work.

It is also possible to vary the reference period by collective or workforce agreement (see page 54). One way it can be varied is to have successive 17-week blocks as the reference periods rather than have a rolling 17-week period. In other words the first 17 weeks after an agreement was reached could count as the first reference period. Another reference period would then start in week 18.

Another variation that can be made is to extend the reference period. Unions in some workplaces have agreed deals that extend the reference period to a year, providing what is known as an annualized hours contract. This allows companies to respond to seasonal peaks in demand in a flexible way but ensures employees get extra time off when demand is slack.

Individual opt-outs

The 48-hour average limit is the one part of the Working Time Regulations from which individuals can opt out. You need to do this in writing and you can opt out either for a defined period of time or indefinitely.

But you have the right at any time to reverse your opt-out so that you can be covered by the 48-hour average limit once again. The longest you can be made to wait before you regain protection is three months. If the agreement you originally signed specifies a shorter period then that will apply.

The commonest abuse of the Working Time Regulations is employers putting undue pressure on their employees to individually opt out of the 48-hour limit. However they cannot force you to opt out if you do not want to and they are committing an offence if they dismiss you or treat you less favourably than other employees – what the law calls 'detriment'. If they do this, you should take advice, as you are likely to have a strong case at an Employment Tribunal. You will almost certainly get compensation, but you should be aware that if you get the sack tribunals only rarely use their power to get people reinstated to their jobs.

However, you are in a more tricky position if asked at a job interview whether you will be prepared to opt out and it is apparent to you that this is a condition for getting the job. This is clearly against the spirit of the Working Time Regulations, but the regulations do not specifically outlaw it, so employers can probably get away with this.

Once you have started work with an employer, however, and have signed an opt-out you can withdraw it at any time. The longest you can wait for that to come into effect is three months. If your employer sacks you at this stage simply for reversing the opt-out he is breaking the law, and you can take a case to an Employment Tribunal.

You cannot have your basic pay cut to punish you for refusing to opt out. However if you are paid by the hour, or receive overtime for hours over your basic working week then you will obviously get more pay if you work more than 48 hours than if you work fewer. There is nothing to stop an employer from paying a higher rate of overtime for hours over 48 hours a week, but if you find your overtime pay has been cut for hours under the 48-hour limit, this may be an illegal variation to your contract of employment. You should take further advice.

Night working

Rights for night workers are easily summarized:

▌ If you regularly work at nights, you should do no more than an average of eight hours in every 24.

▌ Your employer should provide a free medical check, and where possible, allow you to switch to other shifts on medical advice.

▌ Young people and those doing specially hazardous work get better protection.

However, as with other working time rights, they are not so straightforward in practice. Some groups are exempt, and the averages for night work limits are calculated in a different way than for seeing whether you work more than the 48-hour limit.

Defining night work

If you only occasionally work nights, you do not get this protection, only night workers do. To be classed as a night worker you have to work more than three hours at night as part of the normal course of your job. 'At night' means between 11pm and 6am. So if you have an evening shift that finishes at 2am you are a night worker, but if you finish at 1am you are not as you are only working two hours at night.

However, this definition of night can be varied by agreement between the employer and the workers by collective and workforce agreements (see page 54). Agreement can also be reached to include more people as night workers – say everyone who works more than two hours during the night period. But there are limits to how much these definitions can be changed. Night time must always be seven hours or more, and it must always include the time between midnight and 5am.

One of the first court cases under the Working Time Regulations was about the definition of a night worker. The court was asked to rule whether someone who worked one week in three on a night shift was a night worker. The employer argued the worker was not a night worker as she worked days more often than she worked nights, but lost the case. The court ruled she was a night worker and said it was the regular nature of her shift pattern that made her a night worker. However it is likely that other cases will seek to reopen this issue, and you cannot therefore rely on this case as setting a definite legal precedent.

Working out the average limit for night work

Night work is worked out as a daily average limit, rather than a weekly limit. It is therefore calculated differently from the 48-hour limit. It is important to appreciate that the average is worked out over the days you can legally work in a week, not the days you actually work. As you are only entitled to a 24-hour rest period each week this leaves six days when you can legally work.

In other words, you could work nine hours for five nights each week. At first sight this might look as if it breaks the limit of 'a ceiling of an average of eight hours' night work in every 24'. But you have to include the sixth night, when you could work even though you are not doing so, when you work out the average.

Let's look at that calculation in detail. Your total working hours in a week is 45. To get the average over six days you divide by six. This gives seven and a half hours. You are therefore not over the limit. If you work exactly the same hours each week then you can use this method to see whether you are over the limit. But if your hours vary, then it becomes more complex.

The average is always worked out over 17 weeks. Those groups of workers who have their 'reference period' extended to 26 weeks for working out the 48-hour limit (see pages 53, 58) lose night work hours protection altogether rather than have a longer period for working out the average. If you take time off for holidays or sick leave during the 17-week period you assume normal hours are worked on those days.

Overtime is only included if it is a regular part of your work. If you only work occasional overtime it does not count. If, however, you work overtime every week as part of your normal working pattern, you should include it as part of your total working hours.

If you work split shifts – say one week on nights followed by one week on days – your average night hours will be nowhere near eight hours. We can see why by looking at a two-week period. Say you work five days a week and your night shifts are 10 hours long one week and the day shifts, the next week, are eight hours. Over the two-week period you work 50 hours at night the first week and 40 hours during the day the second week, making 90 hours in all.

But, over this period there are 12 days when you can legally work nights. But as you have only done 50 hours of night work during this two-week period the average is 50÷12 or 4 hours 10 minutes a day. You are still subject to the 48-hour limit – but you are also below this.

Special hazards

If your work involves special hazards or heavy physical or mental strain, and you are a night worker, then you cannot work more than eight hours in any 24. This is not an average, but an absolute limit. In other words as soon as you have worked eight hours you must stop. It therefore does apply to split shift workers when they work nights.

But deciding whether your work is covered by this definition may be trickier. Employers and employees together can agree which jobs are covered through a collective agreement – either through union negotiations or a workforce agreement (see page 54). Your employer is also obliged by law to carry out what is called a risk assessment. As part of this he or she should decide whether any night workers fall under this category.

Exclusions from the eight-hour limit

Both the eight-hour average and the eight-hour absolute limit can be set aside in the same way that variations can be made to the 48-hour limit by collective agreement (see the section on varying the 48-hour week above).

The eight-hour limit does not apply to these jobs and workers:

▎ security guards, caretakers and other jobs requiring a permanent presence to protect people and property;

▎ where the job involves long travelling distances;

▍ where the job requires continuity of service or production such as hospitals, prisons, docks, airports, media, post and telecommunications, civil protection, agriculture;

▍ industries where work cannot be interrupted such as utilities;

▍ jobs where there are seasonal rushes such as tourism, post and agriculture.

Any night worker can lose this protection if their job is suddenly affected by an accident, risk of an accident or other unexpected event. But there is no individual opt-out. You cannot sign away your rights. Even if you want to work more than eight hours on average you cannot, unless you are covered by a collective agreement or fall into one of the groups above.

Health checks

Before you begin night work you should be offered a free health assessment. This should be repeated regularly – the government recommends annually. If night work is bad for your health you should, if it is possible for the employer to do so, be offered a chance to transfer to day work.

A health assessment can take the form of a questionnaire, rather than an examination by a doctor or nurse, as long as the questionnaire has been developed by someone medically qualified and is evaluated by someone with training (but not necessarily a doctor or nurse).

Rights for under 18s

If you are over the school leaving age (16) but younger than 18 you are covered by a different set of European regulations – the Young Workers Directive. These were brought into UK law in the Working Time Regulations. Although your holiday rights are the same as older workers, you have different and better rights to breaks.

You should get a continuous break of 12 hours every day (though this can be split in some narrow cases). You should also get a 48-hour continuous break every week (though this can be split in some narrow cases usually involving split shifts, and in some other circumstances limited to 36 hours).

However, as with the 24-hour break enjoyed by older workers, the timing of the break can vary in different weeks. A system where young shop workers got a different two-day break each week would be perfectly legal for example. You could work 10 days in a row if you had two days rest at the beginning of the first week and two days off at the end of the second week. In an emergency, and where there is no adult worker available, these breaks can be suspended but the employer must make them up within three weeks.

From 22 June 2000 young workers won the right under European law to work no more than 40 hours a week on average, but the government has not yet issued the detailed regulations that will bring this into UK law.

Night work and the young

Those who are 18 or under should not work at night, but again the government has not yet issued regulations.

4 *Families and work*

Working parents or those with elderly relatives to care for often find it hard to juggle all the competing demands on their time. Much depends on how flexible their employers are prepared to be, but mothers, fathers and carers also have some basic rights in law.

Working mothers

Working mothers have a range of rights both before and after their babies are born. Maternity rights are very complicated – and the law is not always clear. Here we set out your basic rights, but if you get into difficulties you should check with another source – such as your union or an advice agency. There are contact details at the end of the book. Many employers will provide better rights, which will probably be set out in your contract of employment or staff handbook. They cannot provide a worse deal than the legal minimum even if you have signed a contract that appears to promise less than the law provides.

Pregnancy and maternity leave

The law says employers must not 'unreasonably refuse' pregnant employees paid time off for antenatal care. This is broadly defined and includes antenatal appointments, relaxation and parentcraft classes as well as travelling time. If your employer does unreasonably refuse time off for antenatal care, or if you don't get paid, you can complain to an Employment Tribunal. But the tribunal can only award compensation equal to your pay for the time you took off, or would have taken off.

This is not much use if you did not get your antenatal care. If, however, you do take time off for antenatal care and you are sacked, it is very likely that you could take a case for unfair dismissal. If you are dismissed while you are pregnant your employer must prove to an Employment Tribunal that you were sacked for a reason that had nothing to do with your pregnancy. This is one of the grounds for unfair dismissal that starts with the first day of your job, even if you were pregnant when you started work. You may also be able to claim sex discrimination.

However, a tribunal cannot guarantee that you will get your job back, and you may not get a very good compensation settlement, although this could be more if you win a sex discrimination case. You should take advice before acting from your union or other advice agency.

Maternity leave entitlement

How much maternity leave you can take depends on how long you have worked for your employer. *All* pregnant women employees are entitled to 18 weeks' maternity leave. This is called ordinary maternity leave. As long as you give the proper notice you can take the 18 weeks – it doesn't matter how long you have worked for your employer or how many hours a week you work. You can choose when the leave begins, but the earliest it can start is 11 weeks before the week your baby is due.

But if you are off work for a pregnancy-related reason in the six weeks before the expected week of the birth, your employer can insist that your maternity leave should start from that date. Many employers don't take this line, though, and would let a woman in this position carry on working until she had originally planned to start her leave.

Ordinary maternity leave *must* include at least two weeks after the birth. This is to protect the health and safety of mother and baby.

You get more leave if you have worked for your employer continuously for 12 months at the beginning of the eleventh week before the expected date of childbirth. This entitles you to an extra leave period, called additional maternity leave. This additional period starts when your ordinary maternity leave runs out. You can stay off until the end of the twenty-ninth week after the start of the week of your baby's birth.

Letting your employer know

Whether or not you're entitled to take the additional leave, you have to let your employer know at least 21 days before you start your maternity leave:

▊ that you are pregnant;

▊ the week in which your baby is expected;

▊ the date when you intend to start your ordinary maternity leave.

You should put this in writing if your employer asks you to, and it is probably a good idea to do this anyway in case there is any argument later. Also, if they ask, you should give them a copy of your maternity certificate (MAT B1) given to you by your GP or midwife. If you can't give the 21 days' notice (for example if you had to go into hospital unexpectedly), you must write to your employer as soon as you reasonably can.

Returning to work after maternity leave

If you are only entitled to the 18 weeks' ordinary maternity leave:

▊ You don't have to give your employer notice if you are returning at the end of the full 18 weeks (although it may be a good idea to make sure they are expecting you back if they don't contact you).

▊ Should you want to return earlier than the end of the 18 weeks you have to give your employer 21 days' notice.

▊ Your employer can let you return with less or no notice, but the most they can make you wait is 21 days or until the day that your maternity leave was due to end.

▊ Your employer does not have to pay you if you do turn up for work in the meantime.

If you are taking additional leave:

▌ You don't have to give notice if you are returning at the end of the full period of additional leave (though again it is worth making sure you are expected back).

▌ If you want to return earlier than the end of your additional leave period you should give your employer 21 days' notice.

▌ If you don't give this notice, the employer can postpone your return for 21 days and not pay you if you turn up in the meantime.

If your employer writes to you asking when your baby was born and whether you intend to return to work at the end of your additional maternity leave, you must write back giving this information within 21 days of receiving the request. If you don't, you may lose the right to return to work or to be protected from unfavourable treatment on your return.

However, your employer is not allowed to make this request sooner than 21 days before the end of your ordinary maternity leave period. The letter must also include information about how you calculate the end of your additional leave period and warn you about the consequences of not responding within the 21 days allowed. If it does not, it is not a valid legal request. However unless there is a very good reason, it makes sense to respond to this request.

After returning from ordinary maternity leave you have the right to go back to your old job. You also have this right on going back to work after additional maternity leave – unless your employer can show that it is not 'reasonably practicable' to give you the same job back. In this case, you are entitled to a job that is both suitable and appropriate for you.

Changing your mind about going back to work

You would have to give your employer the normal contractual notice that you are leaving your job. You would not have to pay back any Statutory Maternity Pay (SMP) (see below) you have received, but you might have to pay back any pay your employer gave you over and above the statutory minimum – it would depend on your contract.

If illness prevents you from returning to work

If you are not able to go back after your 18 weeks' ordinary maternity leave because you are ill, you can stay off work for up to four weeks after the end of your maternity leave and still be protected from unfair dismissal. If you are receiving SMP you will continue to receive it for those four weeks. If your employer has a contractual sick pay scheme you should get sick pay for these weeks. If you are too ill to return after a period of additional maternity leave you should receive sick pay from the end of your additional maternity leave. In any case, you should get specialist advice.

Child-friendly working hours

Many women want to go back to work on different, more flexible or shorter hours that are more 'child-friendly'. Good employers recognize this, and either respond favourably to requests or set out your options in your contract of employment. Unions will normally try and negotiate this kind of option for those returning from maternity leave.

There is, however, no explicit legal right to return to work on a different basis. But you can argue that sex discrimination law entitles you to work hours that fit in with your childcare responsibilities. If you make a request to change your hours, and your employer refuses without being able to justify the refusal, this could be unlawful indirect sex discrimination. The law is unpredictable, but there have been successful cases. Take further advice.

Other rights

You have other protections while you are pregnant or on maternity leave:

▌ Your employer can't dismiss you, or select you for redundancy for any reason connected with pregnancy or maternity.

▌ You should not be treated unfavourably in other ways – for example, having to work inconvenient shifts or having your job downgraded.

▌ While you are pregnant, when you have recently given birth, and when you are breastfeeding, your employer has to make sure you are not doing work that would put your or your baby's health and safety at risk.

In addition, you maintain certain contractual rights – which differ according to whether you are taking ordinary or additional leave

Contractual rights during maternity or parental leave

When you are on ordinary maternity leave your contract continues and you are entitled to all the benefits you would get if you were still at work – but not your wages. For example, if you have a company car you can keep it, and your holiday rights will continue to accrue.

Your contract also continues during additional maternity leave or parental leave (see below), but some contractual rights will be suspended until you pick them up again when you go back to work – these could include occupational pension rights and seniority. You will need to take advice, because your employer might provide a better deal. Also, there are some protections for women's pension rights when they are on maternity leave, which you should ask your union representative or specialist adviser about.

Maternity pay and benefits

Statutory Maternity Pay (SMP)

The rules on maternity pay are complicated. You will get SMP if you meet *all* the following conditions:

▌ You have worked for the same employer for at least 26 weeks by the end of the qualifying week (the fifteenth week before the expected week of childbirth).

▌ You are still in your job in this qualifying week (it doesn't matter if you are off work sick or on holiday).

▌ You actually receive at least £67 (before tax) per week in earnings on average in the eight weeks (if you are paid weekly) or two months (if you are paid monthly) up to the last pay day before the end of the qualifying week.

▌ For the first six weeks you get 90 per cent of your average pay. After that you get the basic rate of SMP, which until March 2001 will be £60.20 per week for 12 weeks. The rate is normally uprated each April.

Maternity Allowance

If you are not entitled to SMP, you may still be entitled to Maternity Allowance, also payable for 18 weeks. Maternity Allowance may be payable to you if you have been an employee or been self-employed for a total of 26 weeks in the 66 weeks before the expected week of childbirth (this is called the 'test period'). They need not be consecutive weeks. However, you will also need to meet some complex earnings conditions.

There are two types of Maternity Allowance and different conditions apply to each. Generally speaking, if you have been earning more than £30 a week (including self-employed income) from one or more jobs, you are likely to be eligible. The standard rate for Maternity Allowance is £60.20 a week (until April 2001 when it is likely to rise a little).

Rather than try to grasp the complexities of the conditions, it makes much more sense to simply apply. The Benefits Agency will be able to work out if you qualify.

Other benefits

If you are not entitled to SMP or Maternity Allowance, you may be entitled to other benefits such as Incapacity Benefit or increased payments to your household such as Working Families Tax Credit. The new Sure Start Maternity Grant is avaible to women in low-income households. To check these rights, contact the Benefits Agency, the Inland Revenue or a specialist adviser (for example, a Citizens' Advice Bureau or law centre).

Parental leave

If you are an employee and the parent of a child born or adopted after 15 December 1999, and you have been working for your employer for at least a year, you have the right to take 13 weeks' unpaid parental leave to care for the child.

Some workplaces will have special agreements on parental leave that have been reached between the employer and the union or other workforce representative. For instance, the agreement might set out how and when you can take your leave, or it might include some payment for employees taking parental leave. You should check whether any such agreement applies where you work. If not, you will still be entitled to the basic state scheme.

Where your employer does not provide payment for parental leave, you might be entitled to state benefits or tax credits if you are low paid. You should consult the Benefits Agency, the Inland Revenue or a specialist adviser – your union, a Citizens' Advice Bureau or a law centre.

The basic scheme

You qualify for the 13 weeks' leave if you have parental responsibility for a child or if your name is on the birth certificate (see page 74 for more about who qualifies for parental responsibility). Unlike paid holiday rights, your employer cannot tell you when to take parental leave, but he or she can postpone it. You can take leave at any time:

▌ until the child's fifth birthday;

▌ in adoption cases, for five years after the child is first placed with the family – or until the child's 18th birthday if that comes sooner;

▌ if the child has a disability and is entitled to a disability living allowance, until the child's 18th birthday.

You get the 13 weeks for each child. You have to take the leave in week-long blocks. You can only take shorter periods if your child is entitled to a disability living allowance, in which case you can take leave in periods shorter than a week. You cannot take more than four weeks in any one year for any one child, but, for example, if you have two eligible children you can take eight weeks a year.

You must give 21 days' notice of taking parental leave. You don't have to put this in writing, but it is advisable to do so. The notice has to say when you want the leave to begin and end. If you are the father of an unborn child and you want to take the leave from the date of the birth, you should give notice at least 21 days before the beginning of the expected week of the birth, saying how much leave you want.

For adoptive parents who want to take leave from the date the child is placed with them, the notice period is 21 days before the week of the placement. If that is not practical, you have to tell the employer as soon as is reasonably practical.

Returning to work after parental leave

If you take four weeks or less parental leave you can go back to your old job. But if you take more than four weeks, the rule is that you get your old job back unless it is not 'reasonably practicable'. In that case your employer would have to give you another suitable and appropriate job. This also applies if you add your parental leave on to the end of your additional maternity leave – even if the parental leave was less than four weeks. The job you go back to must not be on lower pay or worse conditions than before you went on leave.

Postponement

Employers are able to postpone employees' parental leave if they think it would disrupt the business. Your employer would have to give you notice of postponement in writing within seven days from the day you give the employer notice that you want to take leave, and you have to be given a reason.

The difference between parental leave and paternity leave

There is no legal right to paternity leave. Some employers do provide time off for new fathers around the birth of their baby – this is more likely where there is a recognized union. A few even provide some time off for employees who are not fathers, but are other partners (eg in a lesbian relationship) or friends on whom the new mother depends.

Strictly speaking, paternity leave should be kept separate from parental leave, because it is partly intended to support the mother around the time of the birth. You should get advice if you already get paternity leave and your employer tries to deduct it from your 13 weeks' parental leave entitlement.

In workplaces where paternity leave is not provided, anyone who qualifies for parental leave can use some of that leave around the birth (see below for an explanation of who qualifies for parental leave). Also, all employees can get 'reasonable' time off for dependants, and this includes time off to take necessary action to help a dependant who gives birth. But take specialist advice before trying to use 'time off for dependants' for paternity leave purposes – this has not been tested in the courts.

Deciding who has parental responsibility

Natural mothers and married fathers automatically have parental responsibility. Unmarried fathers will have parental responsibility if they have been granted it by the mother or through a court order (this will change, as the government intends to amend the law so that unmarried fathers who jointly register the birth with the mother automatically get parental responsibility).

Adoptive parents usually get parental responsibility when the adoption order is made. Same-sex partners or others may sometimes get parental responsibility through legal proceedings.

If you are an unmarried father and your name is on the birth certificate, you are entitled to parental leave even if you don't have a formal parental responsibility order.

If your employer is disputing your right to take leave on any of these grounds, you should take advice from a family lawyer or specialist family law adviser. You can contact the Law Society for details of family law specialists.

Problems

If you think your employer has unreasonably postponed your parental leave or prevented you from taking it, you can take a case to an Employment Tribunal. You would have to make your complaint within three months. If the tribunal finds in your favour it can tell the employer to pay you compensation.

Also, your employer is not allowed to treat you unfavourably simply because you applied for or took parental leave – this would include, for example, harassing you, taking away your company car or taking away job responsibilities. Again, if this happens you can go to an Employment Tribunal. Nor can you be dismissed because you asked for or took parental leave – *that* would be unfair dismissal (see Chapter 7).

Some employers give new mothers more than the legal minimum amount of maternity leave. If your employer tries to deduct this extra amount from your 13 weeks parental leave, this could be in breach of your contract or sex discrimination law.

If any of these problems arise you should take advice from your union representative or other specialist adviser.

Time off for dependants

Quite separately from parental leave, all employees are entitled to 'reasonable' time off to help people who depend on them, such as family members and friends. The time off does not have to be paid, but some employers do give paid leave in these circumstances.

A dependant means your husband or wife, your child or parent, or someone who lives in the same house as you and is not your employee, tenant, lodger or boarder. So, for example, this could include your unmarried partner (of either sex) or another family member or friend who depends on you. A dependant can also be anyone who 'reasonably' relies on you for assistance if they are ill or injured. This might include a friend or neighbour.

You can take reasonable time off for a number of reasons:

▌ to help a dependant if they fall ill, give birth, or suffer assault or injury;

▌ to make care arrangements for a dependant who is ill or injured;

▌ because a dependant has died;

▌ to deal with a breakdown in care arrangements – eg your child-minder is ill, or your elderly parent's carer does not turn up;

▌ to deal with an unexpected incident at your child's school or otherwise during hours when the school has responsibility for the child – eg during a school trip.

You have to let your employer know as soon as possible why you are taking the time off and when you expect to be back.

This legal right depends on what is thought to be 'reasonable' – and the law doesn't provide a definition. It can be difficult to know where you stand if your employer is refusing your right to leave or saying you took unauthorized leave. If this happens you should consult your union or other specialist adviser.

Problems

As with parental leave, if you think your employer has unreasonably refused to let you take the time off you can complain to an Employment Tribunal within three months of the refusal. If you win the case you may get compensation. Also, again like parental leave, you are protected from unfair dismissal and other unfavourable treatment.

5 Common problems at work

In a well-run workplace it should be possible to resolve problems without involving any legal procedures. Responsible employers will not only have proper internal procedures but also foster the kind of environment where it is possible to raise issues informally. Good employers recognize that if their staff have grievances and other problems they are unlikely to give of their best.

But things can go wrong in even the best-run workplaces. Responsible employers may have good policies, but a bullying manager in a branch office may ignore them all. Of course, you should make every effort to resolve issues informally if it is possible. You can talk to your boss or, if they're the problem, your personnel or human resources department. If you have one, your union representative may well be able to sort out many problems on an informal basis.

In this chapter we look at some of the commonest problems where the law sets standards or could have a role in resolving a problem. These are health and safety, stress, bullying, drink, drugs, smoking and problems with your contract. We end by explaining how the law regulates formal procedures for resolving grievances or disciplinary matters at work.

Health and safety

You have a right to work in a healthy and safe environment. There are tough laws to ensure that your rights in this respect are safeguarded. While there is always room for improvement and a need for more resources for enforcement – as some high profile cases such as train crashes sometimes remind us – this country is generally recognized as having a relatively effective health and safety regime. However, while most large companies will understand their responsibilities, this is not always the case in smaller companies. And any death or injury at work is one too many.

Under the Health and Safety at Work Act 1974 your employer must ensure that nothing that happens at work makes you ill or injures you (this is known as the 'duty of care'). This could involve guarding machinery, making sure chemicals you work with are safe, and ensuring you can take breaks when you are tired. It even includes providing adequate canteen and toilet facilities.

Every employer must have a health and safety policy, explaining they will manage health and safety, and who is responsible for what. Your employer must identify the hazards you might face at work, assess the risk these hazards pose and detail the steps that will be taken to prevent those risks.

Many people are confused by the specific legal use of these terms in health and safety. Basically, a hazard is something that could cause you harm, and a risk is the likelihood that the hazard will do so. Hazards can be physical (scaffolding or repetitive work, for example), chemical (eg, asbestos or isocyanates), biological (eg, tuberculosis) or psychosocial (eg, stress).

Under the Act you must cooperate with the steps taken by your employer to protect health and safety in the workplace, to the extent that you are able. So if your employer tells you to work in a certain way because it is safer, they must make it possible for you to do as they say.

You must not endanger fellow workers by your actions or omissions. Basically, this means you should follow the safety procedures laid down by your managers, where they have given you the appropriate tools and resources. You should also avoid anything your employer might describe as 'horseplay' or 'pranks' which could go wrong and cause injury or illness.

There are also 'implied' rights and duties in your contract of employment (see Chapter 1) which can be important in any tribunal or court case. Again, there is a basic duty for your employer to provide a safe and healthy workplace, and for you to pay proper regard in the workplace to your own and your colleagues' health and safety.

No goggles provided

Sheila Robinson and her fellow employees were required to wear eye protectors while at work. Sheila was given goggles, but they were no use because she had to wear glasses. She complained to the safety officer and he said he would approach the company to see if they would pay for special eye protectors fitted with Sheila's prescription lenses. But she heard nothing more about the matter and after more than a year decided that she was left with no alternative but to resign.

Sheila claimed that she had been constructively dismissed and that the dismissal was unfair. She won, though only after an appeal. The Employment Appeal Tribunal ruled that the employer was in breach of their common law duty to take reasonable care for the safety of employees. It was held that this general duty included an obligation to act promptly and reasonably in dealing with safety questions or complaints. It was found that there was no good reason for the employer's failure to respond to the complaint, and so the constructive dismissal was found to be unfair.

Everyone is covered

Statutory health and safety rights are not limited to employees (see Introduction for the difference between employees and other legal categories of worker). Anyone present in the workplace is covered, whether they are an employee or a worker – including agency and sub-contracted workers. Even visitors and others not directly under the control of the employer are protected.

A special government agency called the Health and Safety Executive (HSE) polices health and safety. If an accident occurs or if workers, unions or a member of the public raise serious concerns with the HSE, it will investigate and can order changes to be made. As a final resort it can close a dangerous workplace down and prosecute employers in the criminal courts.

In addition, if you are injured at work because of a failure by your employer to maintain proper standards you can claim compensation in a civil action in the County or High Court (see page

142). Employers must be insured against such claims, and should display the certificate.

Your employer must provide you with information about the risks and hazards of your work, and what they intend to do about them. They must provide you with training (at no cost to you) in how to work safely, and keep your training up to date.

Hazardous chemicals are required by law to come with a Safety Data Sheet setting out what the hazards are, and what can be done to prevent illness and injury. The supplier is legally obliged to supply these sheets to your employer.

What your employer must do

Every employer must conduct a risk assessment, and then follow a legally binding 'hierarchy of control' which lays down the order in which various steps should be taken to deal with risks to their staff or anyone else at their workplace.

Firstly, the source of the risk should be replaced, for example, different machinery, chemicals or processes could be introduced.

Secondly, and only if the first option is not possible or 'reasonably practicable', the source of the risk should be isolated from you and your fellow workers. For example it could be put in a sealed room, or guards could be put on machinery.

Thirdly, if the first two steps cannot be taken, the risk should be minimized, by using less of a substance, or reducing the time you are exposed to the risk.

Lastly, if all else fails, the employer should provide you with personal protective equipment (such as ear-plugs, overalls and breathing apparatus).

Most health and safety law requires employers to take all the steps, which are 'reasonably practicable'. This means that they do not have to use a sledgehammer to crack a nut. It does not mean that if it costs money they do not have to do it, and it does not even mean that if they cannot afford it they do not have to do it. In practice, most health and safety measures pay for themselves in reduced accidents, reduced sick pay and reduced compensation payments.

At a minimum, your employer must:

▌ maintain plant and work systems safely;

▌ ensure that risks to health and safety are avoided when using, handling, storing or transporting substances or articles;

▌ provide information, training and supervision to ensure health and safety of workers;

▌ maintain safe access to and from the workplace;

▌ prepare a statement of general policy on health and safety; ensure that minimum standards are met and bring these to workers' attention;

▌ ensure that there are workforce safety representatives and consult with them so that they can assist in establishing and maintaining health and safety standards;

▌ set up a safety committee to review arrangements if the safety representatives request this.

If a union is recognized in your workplace, the safety reps will be chosen through union channels. Where there is no union, it is up to the employer to ensure there are workplace safety representatives, unless it is a small firm employing fewer than five. Such small companies are still covered by health and safety law, but there is no requirement for safety reps.

Where unions are fully involved in the workplace, health and safety system, accident rates fall by more than 50 per cent. Whenever your employer does something that could affect your health and safety, they are required by law to consult either your safety representative or the workers who are affected. This consultation must be genuine – it must be 'in good time' (legal jargon that means it cannot be left so late that there would be no time to make changes as a result of the consultation), and your employer must take account of your response.

Where there is union recognition, unions can appoint safety representatives who have a right to time off for union training; a right to be consulted and to represent their fellow workers; a right to investigate accidents and a right to be involved in inspections by the HSE or local environmental health officers. They can also require joint union–management safety committees to be set up, which have the backing of the national union – providing them with access to information and back up.

If you have a problem at work regarding health and safety, the first person to contact should be your safety representative. You should be given their name and location when you join the company, probably in a staff handbook or attachment to your contract of employment and it will most likely be posted up somewhere on a notice board.

These rules are general and there have naturally been arguments about how they apply in practice. There is a range of case law, however, which specialist advisers will be able to help you with. We describe some specific issues below.

Special hazards

In addition to these general rights and responsibilities there are many detailed rules and regulations about particular hazards that will affect different workplaces or occupations, such as offshore oil or quarrying. These cover issues such as handling particular chemicals, working with particular machinery, noise at work, or where there is a risk of electric shock. Normally there is a duty to display these or make them available. Although they are often in rather heavy legal language and presented in extremely dull small print, it is worthwhile studying them.

Some of the areas covered by specific legislation (or where legislation is being considered) are:

▌ **Back strain** – the Manual Handling Regulations cover most hazards to the back, including heavy lifting (although there are no maximum weights) – the Display Screen Equipment Regulations cover back problems caused by visual display units (VDUs).

▌ **Stress** – the general duties of employers to care for their employees and to assess risks apply, and the HSC (Health and Safety Commission) is consulting about an Approved Code of Practice as this book went to press (see page 84 for more on stress).

▌ **RSI (Repetitive Strain Injury)** – the Display Screen Equipment Regulations cover using VDUs, and the Management of Health and Safety at Work Regulations cover the need to assess risks (including RSI).

▌ **Noise** – if you are exposed to more than 85dB (decibels) at work, your employer should be reducing the noise levels or at least giving you protection – the Noise at Work Regulations cover the issue.

▌ **Asbestos** – exposure to asbestos kills more people than any other work-related hazard. The Control of Asbestos at Work Regulations set out your employer's duties.

▌ **Temperature** – there are minimum legal temperatures in the Workplace (Health, Safety and Welfare) Regulations, but only guidance about maximum temperatures (in the Health and Safety Executive's *Working in the Comfort Zone*).

▌ **Asthma** – workplace exposure to chemicals that cause asthma is covered by the Control of Substances Hazardous to Health Regulations and the HSC is considering an Approved Code of Practice on asthma itself.

There are also specific requirements relating to the provision of first aid facilities and to the reporting of accidents at work or the occurrence of serious illnesses at work. For more details, contact your union or the Health and Safety Executive (address at the back of the book).

If you work in a unionized workplace, it is likely that the union will have made a number of agreements on health and safety issues over and above the statutory minimum. These might include issues such as lifting heavy weights or the temperature in your workplace.

If you believe that you are being put into a dangerous situation at work and there is a 'dangerous and imminent risk' to you or fellow workers, you have the right to stop work and leave the area. If your employer disciplines you, you can apply for compensation, or reinstatement if you are sacked. Before walking off the job you should, unless there really is no time, raise your concerns first with your safety representative, union representative and/or your manager.

If the worst happens

Despite all the regulations, the work of the Health and Safety Executive and union action, 2 million people are injured at work every year and many more suffer a work-related illness. This is what you should do if you are injured or made ill by your work.

Firstly, report it to your line manager and/or safety representative. Get them to record it in the accident book. If you suffer some specified injuries and illnesses, your employer must tell the HSE. This does not necessarily trigger an inspection, but does allow the HSE to know what is happening in workplaces.

Secondly, or if you have problems with the first step, see your GP and explain how your work caused your injury or illness, and, if you are a member, tell your union. If you are lucky and it is appropriate, your GP or your employer will provide rehabilitation, such as physiotherapy, to get you back to fitness and back to work.

If your injury or illness causes you to lose wages, or causes pain and disability for more than a few weeks, you may be able to claim benefits from the DSS, or compensation from your employer. If the injury was due to criminal violence, tell the police. You may be able to claim from the Home Office criminal injuries compensation scheme.

Stress at work

Stress at work has been described as the new workplace epidemic. Every so often a spectacular case hits the headlines when someone wins a substantial award as compensation for suffering stress at work. But such cases are relatively rare, the more common reality is that workers are suffering in silence as stress levels rise each year. Many factors can add to stress levels. Long hours, exposure to noise, a heavy workload, little or no control over the pace of work and poor management are just some of the common contributory factors.

There is no recognition of stress in UK employment law. But this does not mean that you cannot look to the law for help. Legal cases may be rare, but they should wake employers up to the consequences of ignoring stress in their workplace. The first step is to try and identify the factors that are causing you to be stressed, as some are regulated in their own right.

If long hours are the cause then you should check whether you are working longer than the Working Time Regulations allow (see Chapter 3). If noise levels are a problem, then you should talk to your safety representative. Your hearing may also be in danger, and you should take urgent action.

If the real cause of your stress is your heavy workload then you should talk to your manager to see if he or she can take steps to relieve the burden. Many managers have little idea how long tasks they set can take. You should make sure they do. If they are not prepared to take the issue seriously and try to work through with you what needs to be done, then you should ask them directly to take specific action to reduce your stress level. You are always best advised to put this in writing, or at least take notes of any discussion.

If your manager still refuses to deal with your problem, you should consider a formal grievance procedure if your employer has one (see page 98 for more about grievance procedures).

If your stress gets to the point where it is making you ill or you really feel you cannot cope, you should go and see your GP and explain the problem. He or she will probably be willing to sign you off sick for a period of time. This may well bring the issue to a head. One can hope that this will persuade your employer that there is a serious problem and that something needs to be done about it. On the other hand, they may take action against you for absenteeism or 'under performance' or for some other symptom of your stress.

If your employer takes action against you or continues to ignore your problem, you may have the basis of a court case, and you should seek advice. Your case might be that your employer is in breach of the implied duty in the contract of employment to provide a healthy and safe working environment for you. If you are stressed and tired, you are likely to be a hazard to yourself and other workers.

If you are dismissed, or feel that you simply cannot take any more and walk out, you may be able to claim constructive dismissal on the grounds that the situation made it impossible for you to continue working (see Chapter 7 for more about constructive dismissal). It is, however, hard to win constructive dismissal cases. You will almost certainly need to be able to show that you did everything possible to resolve the issue, including using any internal formal procedures, before you left your job.

Tackling the causes

There is no easy individual solution to workplace stress other than to tackle its causes. Research shows that it is not just the amount of work you have to do that leads to stress, but how much control you have over the pace of your work. Anything which gives you more control over how you work will help reduce stress levels.

This is an area where unions can usually achieve more than workers acting on their own. It is likely that other workers are also suffering. A union can present a joint case and approach the employer without any need for you to be personally involved – which is only likely to add to your stress levels.

Macho-management is often a cause of stress. A workplace where a union has helped foster a spirit of partnership is far less likely to rely on top-down management. Giving employees more control over their own workloads reduces pressure and stress, and usually leads to people working more effectively.

Other problems at work

Bullying

A TUC poll has discovered that 5 million people in Britain have been bullied at work. It can be a difficult issue to deal with, but if you are being bullied at work, either by your employer, a line manager or by a fellow worker, do not suffer in silence.

The basic legal protection you have against bullying, as with stress, is the implied duty in your contract of employment of your employer to protect you from any actions in the workplace which cause you ill health or put your safety at risk. This includes action taken by other workers.

Serious bullying can clearly do both these things. But less serious bullying should also be unacceptable as it can often grow into more substantial bullying if left unchecked. If your workplace has a grievance procedure you should use this. If it does not you should make a formal complaint in writing to your line manager. If he or she is the bully, go above his or her head, or go to your personnel or human resources department if there is one.

If none of this works, you may be able to pursue a claim in court, using similar arguments to a stress case that your employer has failed to provide a safe and healthy working environment.

If the bullying involves an element of sex, race or disability discrimination or harassment then the law is more clear, and you can probably make a complaint to an Employment Tribunal (see Chapter 6).

Drink and drugs

Alcohol and drug misuse can cause a range of problems at work. At one end is the genuine concern that people involved in dangerous or potentially dangerous activities such as driving a train, flying a plane or using dangerous machinery are not under the influence of any intoxicating substance. At the other end is an invasion of individual privacy. What you do in your spare time, as long as it has no effect on your ability to do your job, should not generally be of concern to your employer. If you are having problems with drink or drugs, you should seek specialist help. Some suggestions are given in Chapter 9.

While drugs throw up immediate problems because of their illegality, it is probably true to say that alcohol causes more work-related problems. But both can be a real hazard in the workplace, not just to you, but to your colleagues as well.

Although most people can function perfectly well at their jobs after a glass of wine or beer with their lunch, it is not unreasonable for employers to expect their staff to be clear-headed while at work. On the other hand, they should also realize that stress and other work-related problems can be the prime cause of drink and drug dependency.

Alcohol misuse

Sensible employers will have proper policies for dealing with drink problems. About the worst way of dealing with alcoholism is ignoring it until it is too late. But it is easy for well-meaning colleagues and even management to turn a blind eye as a drink problem deteriorates to the point where the only option is dismissal due to chronic bad health, unreliability or other symptoms of alcohol dependency.

Many still see alcohol misuse as a personal failing – behaviour that shows a lack of moral fibre. In fact, it is often the diligent, conscientious worker who can no longer cope who misuses alcohol.

You will probably know if you have a problem with alcohol. This is a book about your rights at work and you should look elsewhere for advice on sensible drinking, but your employer would almost certainly have a good case for dismissing you for gross misconduct if you are routinely drunk or drinking at work, as long as the rules were applied fairly and uniformly across the workforce.

If your job involves the safety of others, for example, driving a bus, train or plane, drinking will be strictly prohibited in your contract of employment, not just during working hours, but also for a set period before you begin each period of work, as alcohol remains in the body for some time after drinking. If your contract of employment prohibits alcohol, under the Health and Safety Act, you are entitled to a copy of your employer's policy on alcohol in the workplace. If your employer intends to introduce such a policy your employer is required to consult 'in good time' with their workforce, or union representatives, on the implications of the policy and how staff will be expected to comply with it.

However, automatic dismissal is not necessarily the best approach. A better way is for both you and your employer to recognize that you have a drink problem. In return for you seeking treatment or help in giving up or cutting down to sensible levels of social drinking, your employer should be prepared to provide support and some understanding that such problems cannot be solved overnight.

Ideally there should be ways of recognizing and dealing with a drink problem before it causes a breakdown in the employment relationship or leads you to do something that in itself would be likely to result in disciplinary action. If you believe that you are misusing alcohol, you should seek help, before it causes problems with your employer. If you let the problem get worse, it will start to affect you at work.

Some companies have an occupational doctor or nurse, or a welfare officer, who would be able to provide confidential help. If you are in a union, it may be able to help. Otherwise, you should seek assistance from your GP or from one of the organizations like Alcohol Concern, which are listed at the back of this book. They will try to establish why you are drinking too much. Work-related stress or other problems can be a factor that leads to drink problems. As we have seen earlier in this chapter, employers do have a duty of care and should not subject their staff to excess stress. This is one reason why they should not automatically deal with drink-related problems as a disciplinary matter. Poor employment practices may have triggered the problem in the first place.

Drug misuse

Many of the problems associated with the misuse of drugs at work are similar to those associated with the misuse of alcohol and the ways in which you can tackle the problem are also similar

However, the most obvious *difference* is that alcohol is legal, while most recreational drugs are not. Your employer is perfectly within his or her rights to call the police if you are caught in possession of illegal drugs at work. You could be both prosecuted and dismissed for gross misconduct.

The Misuse of Drugs Act 1971 classifies drugs in three categories, A, B and C, according to their relative harmfulness when misused. Class A includes LSD, cocaine, heroin, morphine, methadone, opium, ecstasy and injectable forms of Class B drugs; Class B includes cannabis, amphetamines ('speed'), barbiturates ('downers'), codeine and methaqualone ('Mandrax'); Class C drugs include most sleeping pills, tranquillizers and some of the less harmful amphetamines. Glue and solvents are not controlled by the Act but when inhaled or sniffed cause extreme perceptual distortion and risk of heart failure and brain damage. Most employers would be likely to include solvent misuse under the general heading of drug misuse.

Some employers now use random testing in the workplace to help them to identify drug misuse. If this is included in your contract of employment then your employer can almost certainly dismiss you for refusing to provide a sample. If however, your contract does not permit drugs testing then you are in something of a legal grey area.

If you have worked for more than a year, it may well constitute unfair dismissal if you were sacked simply for refusing to provide a sample for a drugs test. The new right to privacy in the Human Rights Act may also give you some protection from your first day at work. This, however, is a new law and there will need to be some test cases in this area before anyone can be certain that you have any protection in this area. As we said in Chapter 1, you can refuse to provide a drugs sample at a job interview but there is nothing to stop your potential employer rejecting you for the job if you do.

As with alcohol you should ask for a copy of your employer's policy on drugs in the workplace. Depending on the method the employer uses to hold the results of your test, the employer may need to comply with the Data Protection Act. You are entitled to medical privacy so make enquiries of your employer about the security of such information in the processes used by the employer and their testing laboratory services.

If you are unsure about the methods being used by your employer contact your union, your local Health and Safety Executive office or one of the alcohol and/or drugs advice agencies at the back of this book.

Another tricky area is whether your employer can take action against you at work if you are prosecuted or cautioned for a drugs offence committed outside work and when there is no argument that drug-taking has affected your ability to do your job. Whether your employer, the government or unions like it or not, very many employees do take illegal recreational drugs.

Whether you can claim unfair dismissal will depend on a number of factors if you are sacked as a result of a drugs offence outside work. An important one will be the nature of the job you do, and whether your offence will impact on your employer's reputation. To take an extreme example, if your job is promoting an anti-drugs message, then it would be hard to claim unfair dismissal if you are sacked for using drugs. If you are carrying out a routine job, then you may have a better chance. You will need to seek advice.

If you are using prescribed drugs at work which could, if misused, be dangerous, you may want to consider letting your employer know, though you are under no obligation to do this.

Organizations that can give advice on drugs are listed in Chapter 9.

Smoking

Smoking is a notoriously difficult workplace problem. Balancing the rights of smokers and non-smokers can cause rows in even the best-managed workplaces. There can be no doubt that smoking is not just bad for your health, but for anyone who has to breathe your smoke. But those who smoke are usually addicted to smoking and find it difficult to go for long periods without a cigarette. Non-smokers, on the other hand, often find it objectionable as well as potentially hazardous to their health.

Some employers have simply banned smoking, and of course, in some workplaces, for example, where chemicals are used, it is illegal to allow people to smoke. Where employers have banned smoking, they have sometimes met with resistance from those workers who do smoke. Usually, arrangements are made for smokers to go and smoke in a designated ventilated room, or outside. This can cause tensions, though, as those who do not smoke feel that smokers are getting extra breaks and sometimes their colleagues have to cover for them while they are away having a cigarette.

There is some limited legal protection for non-smokers at work. Health and Safety Regulations say that an employer must ensure that non-smokers are protected from other people's smoke, including in rest rooms and rest areas. Case law also favours the non-smoker, as it has been ruled in an important test case that an employer has an implied duty to protect the health of all their workers and if some of them are exposed to cigarette smoke their health will be affected. In one case, the smoker was only smoking in their own room but the smoke was drifting into an adjacent open plan office. An increasing number of employers now put a clause into their employees' contracts saying that they will not be permitted to smoke at work.

The best approach is to combine a guarantee that staff can work in smoke-free conditions with a sympathetic attitude to smokers that gives them somewhere to smoke without harming others.

Smoking – it's not in the contract

Willie Clark refused to accept a smoking ban introduced into his workplace after a four-month notice period. He argued that as he had always been allowed to smoke at work this had become an implied term of his contract. Willie resigned, claimed constructive dismissal but lost his case.

The tribunal found that the four-month notice period was a wholly reasonable period in which smokers can adjust. The employers had acted wholly reasonably in the circumstances. The tribunal said that 'the right to smoke' could not be implied into the contract because there must be an equal right for employees who do not smoke not to be placed in an environment with those who do. The smoking ban was the introduction of a new, reasonable, works rule – and not a breach of contract.

Contractual problems

Your contract of employment sets out the terms under which you are employed. Your employer should not make changes to your contract unless you agree to them. However, if you disagree with them but accept them in practice by following the changes then the law says that you have accepted them and you lose the right to object. So, if your employer tells you that you must now work an extra half-hour a day, you must continue to leave work at your old time if you are to resist the changes successfully. This is because the courts can find a contract to have changed by custom and practice. In other words, if you do your job in a particular way for some time, but then try to go back to working the way set out in writing in your contract of employment you would be likely to lose in any legal process. A tribunal or court would rule that your contract of employment had changed by custom and practice.

Changes to your contract of employment may be made through an agreement between your employer and a recognized union (see

Chapter 1). This may affect you even if you are not a member of the union if the union's agreement covers all workers in the workplace, or all workers on your grade.

If your employer wants to change the terms of your contract, he or she must give you a statement setting out the new conditions and asking you to accept them. If you do not agree and the change is implemented in any case then you can ask a civil court to rule that the employer is in breach of contract and sue for restoration of the original terms or damages. You cannot go to an Employment Tribunal for breach of contract claims, unless you have been sacked as a result (see Chapter 8).

You are only likely to succeed in a claim if the change has fundamentally altered the contract. Examples where the courts would be likely to rule in your favour include reducing your wages or changing your retirement age. An example of a change where you would probably lose any claim would be if you were asked to move to a new type of computer. This would not normally constitute a fundamental change.

If you believe that the change is so fundamental that it makes it impossible for you to continue working, you can resign and claim constructive dismissal although this is always risky (see Chapter 7).

If your employer gives you notice that he or she intends to change your contract, the law will see this as terminating your current contract and offering you a new one. This means that if you do not want to work under the new terms you may be able to claim unfair dismissal. A tribunal is unlikely, however, to find for you unless the changes are pretty radical (see Chapter 7).

A move too far?

Mr Aslam worked for a bank in Leeds on a low salary. His contract contained a clear mobility clause that stated that he could be transferred to any of the bank's workplaces in the UK. Mr Aslam was told to move to the bank's Birmingham branch without notice but he refused on both financial and personal grounds (he was offered no relocation expenses, and his wife had just suffered a miscarriage). The bank asserted that it had a clear right to insist on the transfer under the express mobility clause of Mr Aslam's contract. He resigned, claimed constructive dismissal and won.

The employer argued that they had simply invoked an explicit clause of the contract, but this was rejected. The EAT ruled that employers still have to meet the implied terms in any contract, and in particular when dealing with mobility clauses: reasonable notice must be given before exercising the power to transfer an employee; a mobility clause must be operated in a way to make it feasible (an employee should not be required to do something that was, in practice, impossible). Also, a mobility clause is subject to a general duty not to behave in a way likely to destroy mutual trust and confidence between employer and employee.

In the same way that an employer is not entitled to apply a rule in any way they want, they are similarly not entitled to insist on a contractual right in any way they want. In both cases there is a duty of reasonableness.

Disciplinary procedures

If you get in trouble at work, or your employer thinks that you are not working effectively, it is likely that your employer will start a formal disciplinary procedure. Unless you are guilty of serious misconduct or your employer is unfair, it is likely that this first stage of the procedure will end with you being given a verbal warning. Responsible employers will view a first stage as an opportunity to encourage you to improve your performance rather than punish you.

Employers do not have to have disciplinary procedures in place. But, if they have more than 20 employees, an absence of a proper disciplinary procedure will probably mean they are likely to lose any challenge in a tribunal simply because they do not have fair procedures.

ACAS (Advisory Conciliation and Arbitration Service) has produced a good model disciplinary procedure, which many employers use. You must be told about the disciplinary procedure in your contract, in a staff handbook or in your written statement of employment particulars (see Chapter 1). In the public sector and larger private companies, disciplinary and grievance procedures are almost always available. But some companies, particularly smaller ones, do not have them. A tribunal will accept a less formal procedure in a small company as fair, but will still expect it to allow you to give your point of view and follow some basic principles (see Chapter 8 for more about this).

A disciplinary procedure is usually set out in writing and you should receive a copy of it, or at least be told where you can get a copy, when you start work. Normally, a disciplinary procedure will have a number of stages of increasing seriousness. But your employer can dismiss or suspend you on the spot if you are guilty of a serious offence. Normally, this will be called 'gross misconduct'. Examples of gross misconduct offences are often contained in your contract of employment or the disciplinary procedure itself. They are likely to include offences such as assault, theft and workplace drug abuse.

If you are not accused of gross misconduct the first stage is likely to be a verbal warning. Your manager or another senior member of staff will call you in and tell you that you must improve your performance, or not continue to do something wrong. You could, for example, be told that you must stop being late for work. The warning is usually lifted if your conduct improves. The employer should tell you that the warning is formal and is the first part of the disciplinary procedure.

The next stage is likely to be a written warning, if you do not improve your performance. If the offence is regarded as more serious, your employer may go straight to this stage without giving a verbal warning. The written warning should give details of the complaint against you, the improvement required and the timescale allowed for the improvement. The warning should notify you that if there were no improvement, your employer would invoke the next stage of the procedure. Generally, if there is an improvement, the written warning will be removed from your file after a year.

There may be provision for a final written warning, which can be the last stage before dismissal. This warning must tell you that dismissal is the next stage and also tell you about any appeal procedure. Again, it is likely that the warning would be kept on your file for at least a year.

In addition to, or instead of, a final written warning your employer may tell you to attend a disciplinary hearing. You have a legal right to be accompanied by a trade union representative or official, or a workplace colleague (see below). You are strongly advised to exercise that right and to choose somebody who has had past experience of handling disciplinary hearings in your workplace. If you, or your chosen representative, cannot attend at the time or date given, you have a legal right to ask for a postponement of up to five days, and for a rearranged hearing at a different time and date.

At the hearing, your employer will explain why you have been asked to attend the hearing. You or your representative will then be invited to make an opening statement so that you can explain your behaviour or refute the charge, depending on the circumstances. You will probably be allowed to call witnesses in your support. But you should make sure that they understand why they are being called and what they are being asked to do. You should not ask anyone to do anything but tell the truth, but it is perfectly legitimate to talk through with him or her what he or she will say to ensure it is helpful. You can be sure your employer is doing the same with the witnesses he or she is likely to call. It is important to prepare your case carefully and be sure of all your facts. You should do this with the person who will be accompanying you. Think through what is likely to be said against you and how best you can respond to it.

A formal disciplinary hearing, particularly in a larger company, is likely to be before more than a single manager. It could, for example, comprise a senior manager, the personnel or human resources manager and your line manager or supervisor.

After the hearing, your employer will let you know, probably both verbally and in writing, what has been decided. This could be dismissal, with appropriate notice, or, if agreed by you or provided for in your contract, payment in lieu of notice. Dismissal decisions should only be taken by senior managers. Other penalties might be transfer, suspension with or without pay, demotion or loss of increment, but only if such penalties are allowed for in your contract or agreed by you.

The written notification of the penalty should include the reasons. If you are dismissed and have been employed by your employer continuously for one year or more, you have a statutory right to written reasons for dismissal (see Chapter 7).

In most workplaces where there is a disciplinary system, there will be a right of appeal. You will probably have to lodge your appeal within a certain, probably short, time, often five working days. The appeal should be heard by a senior individual not previously involved in the disciplinary procedure. In a small business this may not be possible. Again, you have a right to be accompanied by your union representative or by a colleague. It is likely that you or your representative will be invited to open the proceedings by explaining why you are appealing against the decision to discipline or dismiss you. You should get a verbal decision, followed by a written decision, on the same day, or as soon as possible after this.

Failure by your employer to use the procedure properly will count against him or her if you make a subsequent claim at an Employment Tribunal and can lead to an increase in any compensation you are awarded. If you fail to attend a hearing, unless it is for good reason, your compensation can be reduced even if the tribunal finds the dismissal to have been unfair (see Chapter 8).

It may be that your employer has more than one complaint about you. If so, each should be treated as a separate issue, particularly when establishing whether they are justified or not. However, if it comes to deciding a penalty for multiple offences it is legitimate for your employer to consider them together.

In practice many employers will put complaints together and deal with them in one procedure and at one hearing. If this is the case, you should insist that each offence be dealt with individually. You should not allow your employer simply to create a general impression of your alleged failures as a substitute for a proper investigation of the facts in each case.

A criminal prosecution outside the workplace should not automatically trigger a disciplinary procedure, though when this can occur may be specified in your contract. If, for example, you are prosecuted and found guilty of an offence against children and you are employed in a job which involves working with children you must expect a disciplinary procedure at work.

A criminal prosecution for an offence committed in the workplace is likely to trigger dismissal for gross misconduct, depending on the nature of the offence. Your employer, however, should not rely on an outside process. He or she should still conduct his or her own investigation regardless of the criminal prosecution. You may be suspended pending the criminal investigation. This should be on full pay until the case is decided, unless your contract provides otherwise.

A fight to the finish?

Jason Green was involved in an argument with his supervisor. During the argument the supervisor questioned the fidelity of Jason's wife, and Jason punched the supervisor. He was sacked. The employer argued that this was an inevitable consequence of striking a superior. But Jason claimed unfair dismissal, and won.

The tribunal did not agree with the employers that dismissal was the inevitable consequence of Jason's action. The degree of provocation should be looked at, and Jason had acted under severe provocation.

However this should not be taken as a green light to hit your boss! There are very few cases where anyone has won an unfair dismissal case after striking a manager.

Grievance procedures

Do not confuse these with disciplinary procedures! Disciplinary procedures, as described above, are used where your employer believes that you have done something wrong, or are not performing well. Grievance procedures are for use where *you* have a grievance or a complaint about something that is happening at work. In other words disciplinary procedures are when your employer thinks you are doing something wrong. Grievance procedures are for when you think *you* are the victim.

There is no legal requirement for your employer to have a grievance procedure. But if there is a procedure, then you must be given information about it when you start work. This can be either in your staff handbook or provided with your contract or statement of written particulars of employment.

You will probably not be entitled to trigger a grievance procedure for a relatively trivial issue, such as being mildly irritated by your neighbour's habit of chewing gum all day. But you should be free to raise any more serious matter. This may be a complaint about something your employer or manager is doing or not doing, or a complaint about the conduct of another member of staff that you believe your employer should stop. Issues that you should be able to raise at a grievance procedure include bullying, impossible deadlines, sexual, racial or any other kind of harassment, or seriously uncomfortable working conditions.

Some grievances indicate the development of serious general workplace issues, relating to health and safety or sex discrimination. Others may only be serious for you. In either case, good employers will take any grievance seriously unless investigation confirms them as minor matters.

Details will differ from workplace to workplace but normally you will need to put your grievance in writing to your immediate supervisor or line manager to trigger the procedure. An effort may be made at this stage by your employer to resolve the matter more informally; indeed, you may have lodged the grievance as a way of underlining its seriousness but with the aim of settling the issues informally. If you think this is a genuine effort then it may be appropriate to cooperate, but, if you think it is simply a time-wasting dodge or a way of excluding your representative then insist on a formal hearing.

If you have a trade union representative they will be able to help and advise you about the best way of bringing a successful grievance procedure. They will also be able to accompany you at the formal hearing, as you have the same representation rights as at a disciplinary hearing (see below for more details).

The formal grievance hearing will probably take place before one or more senior managers, probably with someone from your personnel or human resources department. It will be up to you to make your case. Procedures vary from organization to organization, but you will almost certainly be allowed to present written evidence in support of your case and you may be able to call witnesses. If, for example, you were complaining about the stress caused by a heavy workload then a letter from your doctor would help. If you are complaining about harassment, then, if there are any witnesses, you should aim to call them or present written statements from them. You should receive the result of the hearing as soon as possible. Good practice would be to let you have a written ruling within five working days.

If you are not happy with the result, then you should be able to raise it again with a more senior manager in a kind of appeal stage. Another shorter hearing may well take place, depending on the nature of the grievance. Again, you have the right to be accompanied.

If you still do not get a satisfactory response, in a larger company there may be provision for a further full grievance hearing, involving the most senior manager in the organization or plant, and even a further appeal stage beyond that. Again, in the final hearing and at the appeal, depending on the nature of the grievance, you have the right to be accompanied.

Once you have exhausted your employer's procedures and you are still not satisfied, you may be able to go to an Employment Tribunal or the civil courts. You would normally have to show that your employer had denied you your legal rights or was in breach of your contract of employment, including the implied duties discussed earlier in this chapter.

If you cannot show this, there is little more that you can do, unless your union is able to take the matter up as being one of more general concern to all the staff.

The right to be accompanied

All workers now have the right to be accompanied at a disciplinary or grievance hearing. This right applies to all workers, not only to employees, so it does not matter whether or not you have a contract of employment with your employer or hiring company. You have the right to be accompanied by a trade union officer or representative, or a fellow worker. You do not have the right to bring in a lawyer or other adviser. Union officers and representatives will have been trained and accredited to accompany workers. They are likely to bring valuable experience to any formal proceedings. They can accompany you even if the union is not 'recognized'.

If a union is recognized by your employer (see Chapter 1) it is very likely that there will be an agreed disciplinary and grievance procedure and the union will have full representation rights in relation to its members. This is one of the normal benefits of union recognition, and in some workplaces there are employer–union agreements on disciplinary and grievance issues even where there are no negotiations on pay and conditions.

The legal right to be accompanied at a disciplinary hearing is triggered if the hearing could result in a formal warning, confirmation of a previous formal warning or some other action such as suspension, demotion or dismissal. It is, therefore, widely drawn and it is hard to see how your representative could be excluded from any formal hearing. However, the right to be accompanied does not apply to a more informal conversation with your manager about your conduct.

With grievance hearings, the right to be accompanied only applies if your complaint concerns a legal duty owed to you by your employer, for example, your employer's obligation to ensure that you are not bullied or harassed. In practice it should be possible to argue that any likely grievance may have a bearing on a legal duty, and it is unlikely that any but the most grudging or anti-union employer will try and differentiate between legal and non-legal grievances, although they may screen complaints that they consider to be trivial.

If your employer does not inform you that you may bring a trade union representative or a fellow worker to a hearing, or tries to prevent you from exercising your right, you can make a 'reasonable' request to your employer to be accompanied. If they continue to refuse, you can make a complaint to an Employment Tribunal. 'Reasonable' in this context means that the hearing complies with the conditions above and you make the request as soon as possible after being notified of the hearing. It is a flexible term though and if you have special circumstances, for example, you do not speak English as a first language and need a helper at the hearing, it would be 'reasonable' to request to be accompanied.

6 *Discrimination*

The principles behind the law on discrimination are easy to state. In practice however, this is a complicated area of law.

Even though some anti-discrimination law has been on the statute books for more than 30 years, there is still some way to go. Women, on average, earn less than men, and black people earn less than white people. Despite some progress, people in positions of authority at the top of organizations, and even in middle management and supervisor roles, are more likely to be white and male. Most of those who need the National Minimum Wage and paid holiday rights are women. Laws protecting disabled people from discrimination at work are still new and relatively untested.

If you have been discriminated against because of your age, your religion or because you are gay or lesbian then the law offers you no special protection (although it is sometimes possible to use other legal routes).

What the law says

You have the right not to be discriminated against at work on the grounds of your sex, race or disability. A separate law, the Equal Pay Act, also provides for equal pay between men and women. This chapter outlines your basic rights, but this is one of the most complex areas of employment law. If you run into problems you should always consult your union representative or a legal or other specialist adviser.

Sex and race discrimination

The laws against sex and race discrimination are similar. Your rights are mainly contained in the Sex Discrimination and Race

Relations Acts, but there are also European Union laws on sex discrimination that apply to the UK. The Sex Discrimination Act 1975 says you should not be treated differently just because you are a woman (or a man), or because you are married. The Race Relations Act 1970 makes discrimination unlawful if it is because of a person's race, nationality, or ethnic or national origins.

The good news is that these laws apply to almost everyone at work. They cover you when you apply for a job and from the first day of your job. It does not matter whether you are an employee, a worker, self-employed or a trainee.

If the discrimination happens while you are at work or while you are working for your employer, your employer is liable, even if it is not the employer personally who is discriminating against you.

If you think you have been discriminated against unlawfully, you can take a case to an Employment Tribunal, but you must do this within three months of the incident you are complaining about. You might be awarded compensation. This can include an element to cover injury to your feelings. There is no upper limit on the amount, and some large awards that make the headlines have been won. However, most cases do not result in large awards.

Protection under the sex and race discrimination laws

The sex and race laws protect you against three types of discrimination: direct and indirect discrimination, and victimization.

Direct discrimination occurs if you are treated less favourably than another because of your sex or race. Examples of sex discrimination might include a case where a male employee is offered training, but it is refused to a woman employee 'because she might go off and have a baby'. Another example would be if a man were promoted over the head of a better-qualified woman. A race discrimination example would be where a black person applies for a job and is told it has gone – and then a white person applies and is offered an interview.

If a tribunal rules that you have been treated in a discriminatory way then the employer's motive for discriminating against you does not affect the outcome of the case. For example, when the white owner of a corner shop has hired a black person as a counter assistant, but sacks her when his white customers tell him that unless he gets rid of the black employee they will withdraw their custom. If the shop owner tells the black employee that he hates doing it but she must leave to save the business, he or she is still guilty of race discrimination – because the sacking was on the grounds of the employee's colour.

Similarly, if an employer refused to employ a woman just because she wouldn't like the job because she would not 'fit in' with a long-established, all-male work area, that would still be unlawful sex discrimination. Even where employers don't realize they are discriminating, the unfavourable treatment is still unlawful.

Indirect discrimination is a harder concept to pin down. It happens when an employer sets out 'conditions or requirements' that everyone has to meet, but one sex, or a people of a particular race, cannot meet so easily. If the condition or requirement cannot be justified, then it is likely to be indirect discrimination. You do not have to show that the employer *intended* to discriminate. Here are some examples of how it can happen:

▌ A high level of fluency in English might be a job requirement. This could exclude a higher proportion of black than white workers. If the job was, say, driving a bus with a conductor you could argue that this was indirect discrimination because driving a bus does not require a high level of fluency in English. On the other hand, if the driver also had to collect fares and help passengers on a one-person bus then it would be legitimate to demand higher standards of spoken English.

▌ An employer relies on word-of-mouth recruitment, or gives preference to relatives of existing employees or to internal candidates. Such practices can amount to indirect discrimination if they exclude more women than men, or a higher proportion of people of particular racial origins.

▌ All employees have to work early morning shifts. This could be more difficult for women than for men, because more women than men are likely to have childcare responsibilities.

Indirect discrimination cases are very tricky. You have to prove two different points.

Firstly, you must show that the condition or requirement you are complaining about is discriminatory. You will have to be able to demonstrate that it causes one racial group or sex real disadvantage.

Secondly, you then have to prove the requirement or condition was not justifiable. You will need to show that the employer could drop it, and that it would make no real difference to the effectiveness of the organization.

Victimization occurs when someone is treated unfavourably after complaining about or alleging race or sex discrimination, or giving evidence or information in a sex or race case. For example:

▌ You are demoted because you gave evidence against the employer in a race discrimination case brought by a colleague.

▌ You are sacked after claiming sex discrimination after a failed promotion application.

▌ You are transferred after complaining that colleagues are making racist remarks.

A recent sex discrimination case has highlighted the fact that you can claim victimization *after* you have left your job. For example, when your employer refuses you a reference after you have taken a case against them. Unless the law is changed, though, this only applies to sex discrimination.

Sexual and racial harassment are not specifically mentioned in the sex discrimination and race relations laws – but in many cases such harassment will be covered by the Acts and you could have a case.

Sexual harassment can include inappropriate touching or remarks, requests for sexual favours or other offensive behaviour. Racial harassment can include being subject to racist 'jokes', being ostracized by white workers or being exposed to racist language or graffiti. In extreme cases sexual and racial harassment can amount to criminal assault.

If you are being racially or sexually harassed it is important to make it clear to the harasser that you regard the behaviour as offensive. If possible tell the harasser to stop. Inform your employer. Keep evidence and try to get witnesses. Above all, tell your union representative or other adviser. Remember – your employer has a duty to protect you against such treatment even if it comes from your colleagues – if they don't, you could have a sex or race discrimination case against them.

It's the pattern that counts

Kate White was fed up with the constant stream of sexual innuendo she faced every day at work. Even in an interview with her boss when she was trying to be promoted, he had told her that she would do better with a low-cut dress. Eventually she decided to take action and took a case to a tribunal claiming sex discrimination. Although the tribunal agreed that 58 different incidents of sexual harassment took place, her boss claimed that it was all light-hearted and jokey, and that he commonly made similar remarks to his male colleagues.

The tribunal dismissed her case, on the grounds that none of the 58 incidents were serious enough to count as discriminatory. But she won an appeal. The Employment Appeal Tribunal said the pattern of behaviour should be looked at as a whole and made clear that there is a difference between jokes between male staff and remarks made by a man to a woman.

Equal pay

EU and UK laws give women and men the right to equal pay. Under the Equal Pay Act a woman can claim equal pay with a man who is doing:

▌ 'like work' (that is, work that is the same or broadly similar); or

▌ 'work rated equivalent' under a job evaluation study; or

▌ 'work of equal value'.

The Act covers workers – including apprentices and people working from home – whether on full-time, part-time, casual or temporary contracts. It doesn't matter how long you have worked for your employer. It also covers you if you have a contract to carry work out personally for someone else.

If you are a woman taking an equal pay claim you have to compare your pay with that of a specific man. Your first step, therefore, is to find a suitable man who will be known as the 'comparator'. He does not have to agree to this. This can be difficult as, particularly in workplaces where there tends to be individual salary packages rather than groups all doing the same job, it can be hard to find out how much other people earn. And it's not quite polite to ask! Not everyone can be a comparator. The law says the comparator has to be 'in the same employment'.

Clearly, anyone who works with you and has the same employer can be a comparator. But it can be stretched more widely than this. You can also choose a comparator who works 'at the same establishment' for an associated employer. If this is not possible, you can also look for a comparator at another workplace if the place of work meets two conditions. Firstly, it must belong to your employer (or to an associated employer). Secondly, people must be working on the same terms and conditions. In the public sector this can give quite a wide scope for comparison, but it can be tougher in the private sector, particularly in a small business.

How far you can look for a comparator is one of those complex areas of law where it is very hard to give general guidance. Many cases will depend on precisely this point, and different courts and tribunals have interpreted the law in different ways. Also, EU law lets you make wider comparisons than UK law. This is an area where it is crucial to get expert advice.

Once you have found your comparator there are three ways you can establish you are not getting equal pay.

The first is the most straightforward test. You have to show your comparator is doing 'the same or broadly similar work'. This does not mean you have to be doing identical jobs. They can count as broadly similar as long as any differences between them are not of 'practical importance'. A difference of 'practical importance' could include extra responsibility or additional duties.

The second way you can claim equal pay is by showing that your comparator is doing work that has been 'rated as equivalent under a job evaluation scheme'. This is the kind of scheme that employers often use to set their pay structures.

Normally outside experts with experience of this work and a wide knowledge of how different organizations relate pay to different jobs will carry out the evaluation. They will look at all the different jobs and rate them by different criteria such as the responsibilities involved, the skills required and the knowledge needed. You will probably end up with scores of some kind for each job.

You cannot make your employer carry out a job evaluation exercise in order to make an equal pay claim. But if they have done one and accepted its results then you can bring a claim using this as your evidence.

The job evaluation scheme must also meet certain tests. The court will need to know that it was thorough, with proper tools used to measure each job. It cannot just be a rough ranking of jobs drawn up on the back of an envelope.

The third way of claiming equal pay is by showing that your work is of **equal value** to that done by a man in the same employment, even though his job is different. In some ways you can think of this as a do-it-yourself job evaluation scheme. You have to show that your work is equal in value to that done by your comparator, using the same kind of headings such as effort, skill and decision-making that a job evaluation study would use.

But claiming equal pay for work of equal value is more complicated than showing that you are doing 'like work' or work rated as equivalent under a job evaluation scheme. Again, you have to find your 'equal value' comparator. He must successfully meet the 'in the same employment' test requirements as a comparator who is doing the same job as you. But, you can look much wider, as you need to find a man paid more than you but whose job has the same value even if it is completely different.

Successful 'equal value' comparisons have been made between:

▌ a woman canteen worker and a male shipyard worker;

▌ women fish packers with a general labourer;

▌ nursery nurses with a waste technician and architectural technician; and

▌ a speech therapist with senior pharmacist and a senior clinical psychologist.

The tribunal procedure for claiming equal pay for work of equal value is more complicated than in other equal pay cases. You should not even think of taking an equal value case without taking expert advice.

Disability

The Disability Discrimination Act 1995 (DDA) gives disabled workers some protections against discrimination at work. It prohibits discrimination against disabled job applicants, employees and contractors. It applies to recruitment, promotion, employee benefits, disciplinary proceedings, dismissal, harassment and victimization.

The DDA employment protection does not apply to employers with fewer than 15 employees, workers in ships or aeroplanes, fire-fighters, police or prison officers, members of the Armed Forces, or people who work overseas.

To be covered by the DDA you must have an impairment or medical condition that makes it substantially difficult for you to carry out normal day to day activities. These are defined as mobility, manual dexterity, coordination, continence, ability to lift everyday objects, speech, hearing, eyesight, memory, ability to concentrate and learn and awareness of danger. The impairment or condition must be long term, which is defined as lasting at least 12 months.

A wide range of conditions are covered, for example:

▌ conditions that have a slight effect on day to day activities, but which are expected to become substantial, for example, arthritis, cancer, multiple sclerosis;

▎ conditions that would have a serious effect if not controlled by medication such as severe depression, or by aids such as, for instance, artificial limbs;

▎ conditions that fluctuate such as ME; and

▎ severe disfigurements.

The DDA covers mental illnesses, but people with mental illnesses can find it difficult to establish that they are covered by the Act. To make a DDA claim you have to show two things.

First, you have to show that you have a condition that is recognized by 'a respected body of medical opinion', such as schizophrenia or manic depression. Second, to be covered by the Act, all disabled people have to show that their condition has a substantial and long-term negative effect on their ability to carry out 'normal day-to-day activities'.

One difficulty with the legal definition of 'day-to-day activities' is that it does not include working in a job. You are unlikely to be covered by the DDA if you have a mental illness that only affects your ability to do your job, even though that is precisely the situation that some people with a mental illness triggered by stress at work find themselves in.

Discrimination involves the employer treating a disabled person less favourably than a non-disabled person would be treated. The difference in treatment must be related to the person's disability. For example, a person might be dismissed because their hearing deteriorates to the point where they can no longer answer the telephone. This would be discrimination unless the employer can justify his or her actions. For example, the employer might say that it was necessary for that employee to be able to answer the telephone. But the employer is expected to make 'reasonable adjustments' to solve the problem. In this case the employer could install a minicom or adjust the person's duties.

The idea of the 'reasonable adjustments' is to remove obstacles that place the disabled person at a disadvantage. Examples could be altering premises, changing working hours, allowing time off for treatment, buying new equipment, supplying additional training or even just providing a reserved parking space. What is 'reasonable' depends on the individual case, but you have to take into account how effective the adjustment will be, the cost and the employer's resources. Clearly an employer cannot be expected to make adjustments unless he or she has been informed of your disability and needs.

As with sex and race discrimination legislation, the DDA makes it unlawful for an employer to victimize a person for alleging disability discrimination, bringing a case or giving evidence in a case. This applies whether or not the victimized person is disabled.

The law on disability discrimination is complicated and you should not embark on a case without taking specialist advice. You can take a case to an Employment Tribunal, and claims have to be made within three months of the discrimination you are complaining about. The tribunal can award compensation, including for injury to feelings. There is no upper limit on compensation. The tribunal may also recommend that the employer makes adjustments in the workplace.

Sexual orientation

There is no specific protection in law for people who are unfairly treated because of their sexual orientation. If someone refuses to employ you because you are a lesbian, if you are not promoted because you are gay, if you are harassed at work because you are bisexual, the law is unlikely to help you.

The only exception is in the Armed Forces. Following a judgement of the European Court of Human Rights in 1999, the Government will have to change the law so that a person can no longer be sacked from the Armed Forces just because of their sexuality. The European Court said that this policy went against the right to respect for private life under the European Convention on Human Rights. This might help other lesbians and gays – particularly in the public sector – once the British Human Rights Act comes into force in October 2000.

Good employers do not discriminate and in some workplaces there are agreements negotiated with trade unions that specifically set out the contractual rights that apply to lesbians and gay men. But when problems arise, the only option is to see whether more general employment laws can offer some protection in some limited circumstances. For example:

▌ If you are dismissed just because you are gay, you might be able to claim that this is unlawful unfair dismissal (see Chapter 7).

▌ In some cases, discrimination on grounds of sexuality could be unlawful sex discrimination. This is very tricky and unsatisfactory. According to a recent Court of Appeal case, to make a claim under the Sex Discrimination Act you would have to show that a gay man had been less favourably treated than a lesbian (or vice versa).

▌ Some cases of harassment might contravene the Health and Safety at Work Act or the implied duty in a contract of employment to provide a safe working place (see Chapter 5).

Badge of pride?

Rosie Meredith was a lesbian, and made a habit of wearing lesbian campaign badges to work. Her employer did not like this, and issued warnings and tried to discuss the matter with Rosie. Eventually they dismissed her. Rosie claimed unfair dismissal, but lost.

The EAT held that it was within the employer's discretion to forbid badges which could be expected to be 'offensive' to fellow employees and customers.

Lesbian or gay working parents have some rights. If you have formal parental responsibility you are entitled to parental leave (see Chapter 4). People who automatically have parental responsibilities are mothers, married fathers and unmarried fathers whose names are on the birth certificate. Others with responsibility for a child can apply for formal parental responsibility through the courts. If you want to do this you should consult a specialist in family law.

Lesbian and gay workers also have rights to **time off for dependants** (see Chapter 4). Your partner would come under the definition of dependant.

Lesbian and gay workers do not always get equal treatment for their partners under **occupational pension schemes**. A growing number of private sector schemes do now recognize an unmarried survivor of a scheme member, but public sector schemes are resisting this. You would need to check with your particular scheme.

Part-time work

Part-time work is not defined in law. It is generally taken to mean any hours below the normal full-time hours where you work. Part-time workers have some protection in law against discrimination, both under the Sex Discrimination Act and under new regulations introduced in July 2000, as we explain below.

Part-time workers and sex discrimination and equal pay laws

The Sex Discrimination Act 1975 and the Equal Pay Act 1970 do not mention part-time workers. But most part-time workers are women, and discrimination against part-time workers can often be indirect sex discrimination (we explain earlier in this chapter how to spot indirect discrimination). Excluding part-time workers from pay-related benefits, or paying them lower hourly rates, can in some circumstances be indirect pay discrimination.

There have been some successful cases – but indirect discrimination is always more difficult to show than direct. You have to show that the employer is imposing a 'condition or requirement' that affects more women than men.

For example, your employer might have a rule saying that only full-time workers can get contractual sick pay. If most of the men in your workplace work full-time, and most of the women part-time, that could be indirect discrimination unless the employer can justify the rule. But your claim could fail, for example, if you work for an employer where there are no or very few men and most of the women employees are full-time. In a case like that you could not show that more women than men are adversely affected by the employer's rule.

Other examples of possible indirect sex discrimination claims might be where:

▋ Your employer excludes part-time workers from benefits like private health insurance or a profit-related bonus scheme. If where you work, most of the men work full-time and most of the women work part-time, more women than men would be excluded so a claim might succeed. Or if full-time workers get extra annual leave after one year's service, while part-time workers have to work for two years before getting more holiday. Again, if most of the full-time workers are men, and most of the part-time workers women, you could have a case.

Another way some women have successfully used the indirect discrimination provisions is by arguing that they should be able to come back to work after maternity leave on reduced hours. The argument is that more women than men find it difficult to work full time, because more women than men take responsibility for young children.

But, although some cases have been won on this basis, others have not. There is a clear case for a change in the law, as this indirect discrimination route is very uncertain. You should not think of trying this route, however, without taking specialist advice.

Part-time work regulations

New regulations should make it easier for part-time workers to claim equality with full-time workers without having to enter the minefield of indirect sex discrimination. (But the regulations do not give you the right to work part-time – so, unfortunately, if you are a woman wanting to work reduced hours because of your caring responsibilities the only legal route open to you would be the indirect discrimination one.)

The new regulations are designed so that part-time workers are not treated as second class when it comes to pay and non-wage benefits. They only became law in July 2000, so there is as yet little experience of how the courts will apply them in practice.

In order to bring a case you need to show that you are being treated less favourably than a full-time worker who the law accepts as a valid comparator, and this is because of your part-time status. Most workers are covered. It does not matter whether you are temporary or full-time, an employee or a worker. The right starts from your first day at work. As long as there are workers doing a similar job, working longer hours than you, and getting better treatment then you can bring a case.

While only employees can claim unfair dismissal if they are sacked for making a claim, everyone is protected against what the law calls *detriment* – such as being passed over for promotion – because you have claimed your rights or helped a colleague to claim under this new law.

The regulations are broad in their scope and almost any term or condition is covered including:

▌ overtime pay (once the part-time employee has worked more than the normal full-time hours);

▌ contractual sick pay;

▌ access to any occupational pension scheme;

▌ training;

▌ holidays;

▌ maternity leave, pay and parental leave;

▌ access to career break schemes.

Who can you compare yourself with?

To be able to claim your rights under the new law you have to show that your treatment has been less favourable than that of a full-time worker. But you cannot compare yourself with just any worker.

It has to be:

▌ a full-time worker, working for the same employer, in your own workplace;

▌ working under the same type of contract as you; and

▌ doing the same or similar work to yours.

If there is no full-time worker at your workplace who matches this description, you can choose someone from another of your employer's locations.

If you have been working full-time and shift to part-time work you can also compare your treatment with that which you previously enjoyed when you were full-time. For example, if you have taken maternity leave and it is agreed that you return to the same job but part-time, you should be able to keep your existing terms and conditions, pro-rata to your working hours, unless your employer can justify the difference. You have this right to compare your situation to the one before you went on maternity leave provided you were not off for more than 12 months.

As long as there are full-time workers in your workplace doing generally the same work, you will be covered. If not, you will also be able to compare yourself with full-time workers at another location, provided they have the same employer as you and are doing broadly similar work to yours.

But it is important to note that your full-time comparator must have the same type of contract as you. This means that if you are part-time and employed on a casual basis, you cannot compare yourself to a full-time permanent employee.

Writing to your employer

Once you have found the eligible full-time worker (your comparator) who is being treated better than you, you should write to your employer and ask why you are being treated differently. Before you do this however, you should talk it through with an adviser, from your union if possible.

Once your employer has your letter, they have to reply within 21 days. If they do not, a tribunal can take this as evidence that your rights have been breached.

You will need to discuss their reply with your union or other adviser, to see if an Employment Tribunal is likely to accept their arguments or side with you.

7 *Getting the sack*

Dismissal

About the worst thing that can happen to you at work is losing your job. The legal term for getting the sack is dismissal. Your employer will tell you that you are no longer wanted, and that from a certain date your employment will come to an end. At the end of this chapter you will find the dismissal maze. This is a table that will help you through the concepts in this chapter.

A dismissal can take place in a number of ways:

▌ Your employer can terminate your contract.

▌ Your job can be made redundant.

▌ Your employer can decide not to renew a fixed term contract.

▌ Your employer can claim that you have dismissed yourself by your actions – either misconduct by you or your inability to do the job competently.

▌ Or, in some circumstances, you can leave and claim that you were 'constructively dismissed'.

Notice

Your contract will normally say what notice your employer is required to give you if he or she intends to dismiss you. It will also normally say what notice you must give if you want to leave your job. But the law does set out minimum standards for periods of notice and your contract must not give you any less than the following. Your employer must give you at least one week's notice after one month's employment, two weeks' notice after two years' employment, three weeks after three years, and so on up to 12 weeks after 12 years or more. Most employees are entitled to receive payment during this statutory notice period. If you are not given adequate notice of dismissal, you can sue the employer for 'wrongful dismissal' in a court or tribunal (see below and Chapter 8).

Once you have had your job for more than a month you must give at least one week's notice. This does not increase, and however long you have held your job the longest notice period you can be made to give is one week.

Employers and employees can waive their right to notice or agree to a payment instead of receiving a period of notice (often called a payment in lieu of notice). The law only allows such a payment if you agree to it or if it is allowed by terms in your contract. If your employer is keen for you to leave immediately you may be able to use this to increase the payment you are given.

Either you or your employer can terminate the contract of employment without notice if the conduct of the other justifies it. You should only walk out if you believe that your employer is acting so badly that you can make a successful claim for constructive dismissal (see below). Although you may be so desperate that you want to just quit on the spot, you should, if possible, take advice as to whether you have a good case. If you do walk out your employer may deduct a week's wages from what is owing to you as you have not given notice. You would have to win a constructive dismissal case to get this back.

If your employer sacks you without notice, it has to be for a substantial reason. If, for example, you have been found guilty of gross misconduct, such as violence in the workplace, race discrimination or theft, then your employer is very likely to ask you to leave the premises immediately. Most contracts of employment will specify circumstances under which the employer may dismiss the employee without giving notice.

Written statement of reasons for dismissal

Once you have held your job for a year, your employer must give you a written statement of why you have been dismissed if you ask for it. The law says this must be given in response to either a written or verbal request, but it is always a good idea to put any communication with your employer about issues such as this in writing and keep a copy. The employer must provide this 'written statement for reasons of dismissal' – its legal name – within 14 days of your request.

If you get the sack while you are pregnant or on maternity leave then you should be given a written statement automatically. You should not have to ask for it and you should get one, however long you have worked for your employer. If you do not get one, you will have a very strong tribunal case.

Constructive dismissal

A constructive dismissal is one where your circumstances become so difficult for you that you are convinced that you have no alternative but to leave. This can occur for, example, if your employer makes major changes to your contract, or your job, without your consent and you find the changes unacceptable. You must exercise great caution in resigning in this way as it is extremely difficult to satisfy a court or tribunal that the circumstances made it impossible for you to continue. Even if you do convince the court, you will probably not get your old job back but will get compensation – which can be modest – instead.

Wrongful dismissal

A wrongful dismissal is a dismissal that is in breach of your contract of employment, or goes against something provided for in your contract. It is not the same as an unfair dismissal, which is explained below on page 120.

Wrongful dismissals can include:

▐ a dismissal without proper notice;

▐ failure to pay your wages in full during the notice period; or

▐ any other breach of the provisions in your contract about notice.

As a claim for wrongful dismissal is a breach of contract claim, you can pursue your complaint in either the civil courts or an Employment Tribunal. The advantages of the court route are that damages are unlimited if you make your claim in the High Court (or Court of Session in Scotland). You can also make a claim in the County Court (or Sheriff's Court in Scotland) if you are claiming less than £25,000.

This is the same upper limit as in an Employment Tribunal, but a claim for wrongful dismissal to an Employment Tribunal must be made within three calendar months of the dismissal occurring. For the civil courts there is a six-year period following the dismissal during which you can make a claim (five years in Scotland).

The disadvantages of using the civil courts are that you will need legal representation and the costs of losing could be high, if your former employer's costs are awarded against you. Employment Tribunals are more informal, and costs awards are not normally made. You should take detailed advice about the best way to pursue a wrongful dismissal claim. It is hard to generalize, but it is likely that only high earners are likely to be advised to take the riskier, though potentially more rewarding, route of a claim in the civil courts.

Unfair dismissal

If you are unfairly dismissed you can take a case against your employer. If you have been dismissed and have also been discriminated against on the basis of sex, race, disability or trade union membership you can claim discrimination *and* unfair dismissal, which may result in higher compensation.

To work out whether you have been dismissed unfairly, it is easiest to explain what the law considers a fair dismissal. If you have not been dismissed fairly then you must have been unfairly dismissed.

Other than in some special cases set out on page 126 in the section on qualifying conditions, you must have worked for your employer for more than a year to gain protection against unfair dismissal. You must also normally get your claim in within three calendar months of getting the sack.

Fair dismissal

A fair dismissal is one that takes place for the following reasons:

▌ your conduct;

▌ your capability or qualifications for the job;

▌ redundancy (your job is no longer needed);

▌ a legal requirement that prevents the employment being continued;

▌ some other substantial reason that could justify the dismissal.

Conduct

Conduct covers your behaviour both on, and, in some cases, off, the job. For a dismissal on grounds of conduct to be considered fair, your employer would generally need to be able to show that they have conducted a proper investigation into your alleged misconduct and given you a chance to answer the case in a properly convened disciplinary hearing. The Employment Relations Act 1999 gave everyone involved in a disciplinary or grievance hearing the right to be accompanied by a fellow employee or a trade union representative, even if the employer does not recognize the union (see Chapter 5).

Some allowance is made for small businesses when considering the procedures used, as tribunals will expect higher standards from companies with full-time personnel officers. But small firms will still need to be able to show that they have established the facts of the case and given you a chance to respond with representation if you wish.

Your misconduct must also be sufficiently bad to justify dismissal. Misconduct outside the workplace can be grounds for a fair dismissal. For example it is likely that a tribunal would find dismissal of someone employed as a driver for a driving-related offence in their own car to be fair, but not the dismissal of someone who does not drive as part of their job. In other words dismissal for an off-the-job offence must be shown to relate in some way to your job.

Clocking out for good

Frank Jones had worked for a biscuit firm for 22 years. He was sacked for clocking in for a workmate, who had slipped back to the cloakroom to collect a cap that he had forgotten but which he had to wear for work. The employees' handbook listed clocking in offences as among those regarded by the company as 'breaches of regulations and will result in instant dismissal'. There was also a notice above the clock that said 'It is a serious offence to stamp another employee's time card. Any irregularities on the card must be reported immediately. Failure to do so means instant dismissal'. The last two words were written in large letters. Frank was seen falsifying the clock by witnesses and admitted to it.

Frank claimed unfair dismissal. His argument at the tribunal was that dismissal was too draconian a penalty after 22 years' service, and that a warning would have been more appropriate. But he lost. The tribunal decided that the dismissal was fair as all staff had been given plenty of notice that a clocking in offence would result in dismissal.

Tribunals have generally treated clocking in offences with great severity. They have, on the whole, accepted employer arguments, reflected in many works rules, that clocking offences warrant instant dismissal. On the other hand, you may have a case if you can show that other workers were treated differently after committing the same offence, or that fiddling clock cards has been a common practice which everyone has previously ignored.

More people succeed in Employment Tribunal cases by showing that their employer has failed to carry out fair procedures than by getting a tribunal to agree that their employer has over-reacted to misconduct. This is because the legal test they apply is whether a *reasonable employer* would dismiss a member of staff on these grounds. This is not the same as asking whether the misconduct is serious enough to justify dismissal, but whether other employers would do the same.

See Chapter 8 for more about Employment Tribunals and their procedures.

The pub lunch

Sid French worked on a passenger ferry. During one of his shifts he went to a pub to have lunch. He was joined by two workmates. The employers had a strict rule that employees should not enter licensed premises while working. A manager went to the pub and immediately suspended all three employees. There was no suggestion that Mr French was drunk – he had merely gone to the most convenient place to obtain food – but his two colleagues acted in a way consistent with their being drunk. On the following day all three were summarily dismissed.

Management argued that as all three had broken the same rule, all three must be punished equally. But Sid claimed unfair dismissal and won.

The tribunal took the view that there were enough differences between the conduct of Mr French and that of his colleagues to make a reasonable employer distinguish between them. To treat all employees the same as a matter of course, without considering the particular circumstances of each individual, simply should not be done.

Many employers try to argue that there are some offences that warrant automatic penalties – no excuse being accepted. This case reinforces the argument that each individual case needs to be considered, and you should have the right to present your case in a disciplinary hearing.

Capability

The second ground for fair dismissal is capability. For the first year of your job you do not have any protection against unfair dismissal (except in the limited circumstances set out on page 126) so your employer can sack you easily if they do not think you are up to the job for the first 12 months you work for them. Once you have worked for more than a year, your employer will need to be able to show that they have followed proper procedures that establish that you cannot perform your job competently.

The most common reason for a fair dismissal in these circumstances is when your health deteriorates to the point that you cannot do your job any longer. However, your employer would need to show that they could not make changes in your working environment that would allow you to continue to work. The Disability Discrimination Act may be relevant in some cases (see Chapter 6).

If your employer has a disciplinary procedure then they must use this to show you are incapable of doing your job. Although there is no legal requirement for an employer to have a disciplinary procedure, they will find it almost impossible to defend an accusation of unfair dismissal in a tribunal if they cannot show they have a proper and fair process.

Redundancy

You are made redundant if your job is ended. Legally, it is the job that is made redundant, not the worker. This is a complex area covered in more detail on page 129. If you are one of a group of workers, doing more or less the same job, and only some of you have been selected for redundancy then your employer must be able to show that the workers to be made redundant have been chosen fairly.

Dismissal on the grounds of redundancy will be deemed unfair if the employee is selected for redundancy when others in the same circumstances are not on grounds of:

▌ trade union membership or activities;

▌ taking certain types of action in relation to health and safety, for example, refusing to do a job where the employee is convinced that there is a serious risk to his or her health and safety;

▌ any reason in connection with maternity;

▌ asserting a statutory right, for example, asking to be paid the National Minimum Wage;

▌ refusing to do shop or betting work on Sundays (see Chapter 5);

▌ acting as an employees' representative in relation to consultation on redundancies or a business transfer;

▌ performing any duties relating to an employee's role as an occupational pension fund trustee.

Dismissal on the grounds of redundancy may also be unfair if your employer has not given you adequate warning of it or if they have failed to consider offering you another job.

Legal requirement

A typical example of this would be getting the sack from a job as a driver because you have lost your licence. However, your employer must also show there is no alternative employment with the company.

A justifiable and substantial reason

This fifth basis for a fair dismissal causes real difficulties as the phrasing is vague. Tribunals have devised various tests that they use when they come to consider whether or not a dismissal was for a 'justifiable' and 'substantial' reason. But at the end of the day the tribunal has to make a judgement as to whether or not the facts of the matter justified the action of the employer. They will consider whether or not any grievance or disciplinary procedures were properly used, or indeed whether or not procedures existed. In these circumstances, it is particularly important for employees to ensure that they have the statutory written reasons for dismissal, as described above.

If the employer can show that the reason for the dismissal was one of those listed above, the tribunal will consider whether or not the employer acted reasonably by dismissing you rather than taking some other course of action.

Shifting a shift?

Two security men, Ron Brown and John Pollard, were asked to change shift patterns as their employer thought this would lead to more efficient use of staff time. After consultation both refused but were sacked. Ron had only been with the firm less than a year so could not make a claim but John was a long-service employee, and his wife was currently ill. He claimed unfair dismissal, but lost.

The tribunal agreed that their refusal to change their shift patterns did harm the business interests of their employer. John's dismissal was therefore a potentially fair dismissal under the category 'some other substantial reason'. This shows that in some circumstances you cannot rely on your contract of employment.

The tribunal will usually concentrate on whether the employee was 'reasonable' in resisting change, and whether the employer was 'reasonable' in insisting on the change. If the employer can show an overriding business need for the change then the tribunal will tend to decide in the employer's favour.

Qualifying conditions

If you think you have been unfairly dismissed you may complain to an Employment Tribunal. In most circumstances, you must be an 'employee' (see Chapter 1) and have worked continuously for one year for the same employer. Members of the police force and Armed Forces cannot claim unfair dismissal.

This qualifying period of one year is not always necessary. It is reduced to one month where you are dismissed on medical grounds because of some health and safety requirements. There is no length of service requirement at all to make a complaint of unfair dismissal if you are sacked because:

▌ You are pregnant, or for any reason connected with maternity.

▌ You are a trade union member or because of trade union activity (or because you have refused to join a union).

▌ You have taken some action to enforce your workplace rights – 'seeking to assert a statutory right' in legal jargon. A common cause is asking to receive a written statement of employment particulars after two months of employment.

▌ You have refused to do something on health and safety grounds (see page 83 for details on what you can and cannot refuse to do).

▌ You have 'blown the whistle' on malpractice in the workplace (see page 24).

▌ You have refused or are proposing to refuse to do shop work or work connected with betting on a Sunday.

▌ You are acting as a representative of employees for consultation on redundancy or a business transfer, or have put yourself forward as a candidate to do this. This might happen in a workplace where there is no recognized trade union as, in some circumstances, an employer must organize elections for workforce representatives so that they can consult with their staff.

▌ You are an employee pension fund trustee or proposing to become one and have been sacked because of your role.

▌ You have represented a fellow worker at a grievance or disciplinary hearing, or because you have asked to bring a fellow worker or a trade union representative with you to such a hearing.

▌ You have campaigned for or against statutory trade union recognition.

▌ You have taken part in lawful industrial action and have been dismissed for doing so within the first eight weeks of that action.

You must make a complaint of unfair dismissal to a tribunal within three calendar months of the 'effective date of termination' of your employment (usually the date of leaving the job). Tribunals do have the power to consider claims made late if they consider that it was not 'reasonably practicable' to get the claim in on time, but in practice they are very reluctant to do this. In particular, waiting for the conclusion of a grievance or disciplinary hearing is not accepted as a reason for delay. It is always best to get an application in early, even if you subsequently withdraw it.

Tribunal procedures are explained in more detail in Chapter 8, which also sets out a number of alternative ways of settling a case, once you have made a claim, that do not involve the stress of a full hearing, and these are certainly worth considering.

If you do proceed to a hearing for unfair dismissal a tribunal will first establish that the dismissal of an employee has occurred. It will then consider whether it was fair or unfair. If it decides the dismissal was unfair it will then decide what to do about it.

There are three possible remedies a tribunal can order. These are reinstatement, reengagement or compensation. Orders for reinstatement or reengagement normally include an award of compensation for the loss of earnings in the period between the dismissal and the reinstatement (see Chapter 8 for more details). The difference between reinstatement and reengagement is that reinstatement gives you your old job back, while reengagement gives you a different, but comparable job.

To be able to claim unfair dismissal, you must not be over the 'normal retiring age'. This is 65 unless a lower retirement age generally applies in your workplace. This means that if your employment contract states that the normal retirement age for you is 60 then you cannot make a claim for unfair dismissal after you have reached 60.

There is no specified lower age limit for claiming, although it is illegal to work when you are under 13. Those defined by their employers as 'apprentices' cannot be dismissed unless their contract specifically says that they may be.

Non-UK companies

The law has recently changed, allowing you to claim if you are employed outside the UK but normally resident here. The law has changed too recently to know yet how this might work in practice. It may well turn out to be difficult to take action against firms based outside the UK.

There are special regulations relating to those employed off-shore, that is, on ships or oil rigs. UK workers posted in EU countries are entitled to all the employment protection that applies to nationals of the particular country in which they are working. This area of the law is complex. If you are working abroad or working in the UK for a foreign-owned company you should take further advice from your union or one of the sources listed at the end of the book about making a claim for unfair dismissal.

Redundancy

Redundancy is sometimes used as a polite word for getting the sack, but it has a precise legal meaning and you have special rights if you are made redundant. In particular many have a right to redundancy pay. A redundancy is a dismissal caused by the employer's need to reduce his or her workforce. It may come about because a workplace is closing down, or because fewer employees of a particular kind are (or are expected to be) needed.

Normally, your job must disappear. It is not a redundancy if your employer immediately takes on someone else to do your job. This does not mean your employer cannot take on workers of a different type, or at some other location (unless the redundant employees could be required under their contracts to move to the new location). But it is still a redundancy if someone else already working for your employer moves into your old job as long as there is an overall loss of jobs. Providing some jobs end, your employer can shuffle existing staff between different jobs and functions.

Your employer must make a lump sum payment to you if you are made redundant, as long as you have at least two years' continuous service with him or her (excluding any service before the age of 18) and meet some other conditions.

In particular, you may not be redundant if your employer, an associated employer or another employer who takes over the business, offers you another job. But they must offer you a new job before your old contract expires and it must start within four weeks. However, the job must be suitable. You can turn down an alternative offer that is clearly unsuitable, or agree to try it out for a four-week trial period. You can agree with your employer to extend the four-week period in writing if you are being retrained. If at the end of the trial period you are still in the job, you will be deemed to have accepted it. This means that you lose any rights to claim redundancy.

If you reject the new job before the end of the trial period, because it turns out to be unsuitable as an alternative, or for good personal reasons, your redundancy will be considered to have started the day your old job ended. However, if your employer disagrees with your decision that the job is not suitable you may need to make a claim in a tribunal and show them why the job was not suitable. If they find you have refused a suitable offer of alternative employment you lose your right to a redundancy payment.

Redundant?

Liz Acott was a lecturer at a college of further education. Her appointment was for one academic year, and was not renewed. This was not a surprise. There had always been doubt that there would be enough money in her department's budget to renew her contract at the end of the period of appointment. But when her appointment was not renewed Liz claimed for unfair dismissal.

The tribunal said that Liz's job was redundant, and redundancy can be a fair reason for dismissal. But they also held that the employer had a duty, as in any other redundancy situation, to try to assist Liz by considering her for other jobs they might have available. Since there was no evidence that the college had done this, she won her case.

What can you get?

The law provides a legal minimum for redundancy pay. Some employers will offer better terms, and some will include these in your contract of employment. The legal minimum depends on the length of your continuous service with your employer, how old you are and how much you are paid:

▌ For each complete year of employment after your forty-first birthday but before you turn 65 you should get one and a half week's pay.

▌ For each complete year of employment after your twenty-second birthday but before you turn 41 you should get one week's pay.

▌ For each complete year of employment while you were either 18, 19, 20 or 21 you should get half a week's pay.

But, unless your employer or contract of employment is more generous, you cannot claim more than 20 years' worth of redundancy payments.

If you are made redundant you are entitled to a minimum period of notice. This is one week for every year you have worked for your employer up to a maximum of 12 weeks. If your employer makes, or lets, you leave before this minimum period of notice you should still be paid for the full notice period.

Working out how many years of service you have in order to calculate your redundancy payment is far from simple. The period starts with your first day with your current employer, and ends at what is called the 'relevant date'. This is the day on which your redundancy notice expires, even if your employer has let, or made, you stop work in the meantime.

It is calculated in calendar years, but with no fractions of a year. If you have worked for 10 years and 11 months, then it is counted as 10 years. The period must be of continuous employment. Days on strike do not count but do not break the continuity of the employment. Periods of maternity or parental leave do count and do not break the continuity of employment. Other absences may sometimes count towards a period of continuous employment, even where the employment contract was broken, for example, by a temporary stoppage of work.

Calculating a week's pay

Working out your years of employment is only the first stage. You can then work out how many weeks' wages you should get. But not everyone is paid the same each week. There could be other arguments about which week to take and which part of your wages count.

The week's wage is taken to be what your contract of employment said you should have been paid in the week your employer gave you notice, for that week's work. If for some reason your employer did not give you formal notice, then it is the week in which he or she should have given you notice.

If your pay varies, for example, if you are paid on a piece-work basis, the amount is averaged over the 12 weeks immediately before the calculation date. Overtime and other bonuses only count if you are guaranteed them in your contract of employment.

But there is an upper limit of how much your weekly pay can be taken to be for the purposes of working out your redundancy pay. The limit is currently £240. It is uprated each year in February, usually in line with the Retail Price Index.

If you are within 12 months of your sixty-fifth birthday, your entitlement is reduced by one-twelfth for each complete month after your sixty-fourth birthday. This reduces your entitlement to nothing by the age of 65.

Your employer may offset part of your company pension payment against your redundancy payment if you are dismissed not more than 90 weeks before the first pension payment is due.

You do not have to pay tax on a Statutory Redundancy Payment and it does not affect your right to claim unemployment benefit. You will not be entitled to Statutory Redundancy Pay if any of the following apply:

▪ Your employment ends on or after your sixty-fifth birthday.

▪ You work for a company with a normal retirement age of less than 65 and you have reached that age.

▪ You are an apprentice whose service ends at the end of your apprenticeship contract.

▪ You are on a fixed-term contract of more than two years' duration which includes, with your written agreement, a clause waiving your right to a redundancy payment, provided your employment ended at the appointed time.

▌ You are a domestic servant working in a private household and you are a member of the employer's immediate family.

▌ You are a share fisherman paid solely by a share of the catch.

▌ You are a crown servant or employee in a public office or in the NHS covered by other redundancy arrangements.

▌ You are an employee of the government of an overseas territory.

If your employer cannot pay because of serious financial problems, the Department of Trade and Industry (DTI) will pay you directly. They will only ever pay the statutory minimum amount even if your contract of employment promised you more. If your employer is insolvent, the payment is made by the DTI and the debt is recovered from the assets of the business. If you have lost out because of a difference between the statutory minimum and what your contract offered you can make a claim against the remaining assets of the company. In order to get payment from the DTI, you must first have submitted a claim to the employer in the normal way, as described below.

Liability for making the payment rests with your employer. It should be made at, or soon after, the time of your dismissal. There is no need for you to make a claim, unless your employer fails to pay or disputes the entitlement. Where this happens, you should make a written request to your employer or refer the matter to an Employment Tribunal, or both, within six calendar months of the date your employment ended. If you do not claim within six months you may lose the right to a payment but the tribunal has discretion to extend this period by a further six months if you make a claim within those six months.

Consultation on redundancy

If your employer intends to make more than 20 people redundant over a 90-day period, he or she must, by law, consult the workforce. If your employer recognizes a union, it must be consulted. If not, your employer must establish a representative body, or make use of an existing representative body, for example, a staff council, elected by the entire workforce.

The agenda for consultation should include ways of avoiding redundancies or of reducing the numbers affected. Agreement does not have to be reached as a result of the consultation but the employer must consult 'in good faith', that is, with a view to reaching agreement. Certain information must be disclosed to the representative body including:

▎ the reasons for the redundancies;

▎ the numbers and descriptions of those affected;

▎ the proposed method of selecting those to be made redundant, for example, 'first in, last out';

▎ how any redundancy payments better than the legal minimum will be worked out.

Consultation cannot just take place one afternoon when the managing director has a spare half-hour. There are minimum periods during which representatives must be consulted. These are if 20 to 99 employees are to be dismissed at one establishment over a period of 90 days or less, consultation must last at least 30 days, and, if 100 or more employees are to be dismissed as above, consultation must last at least 90 days.

Individual notices of redundancy should not be issued until there has been sufficient consultation in line with these requirements. Any complaint that redundancy notices have been issued before consultation ends can be made to an Employment Tribunal. If the tribunal finds that a complaint is justified it can make a protective award, which will require the employer to pay the employees their normal pay for the period covered by the protective award. This is to allow for the consultation to take place before the redundancies are made.

Follow a path through the dismissal maze to find out your basic rights:

Are you an employee? Not all workers are employees. As well as the obviously self-employed, other workers can find that they are not employees in the strict legal sense — see Introduction.	>No>	There's probably nothing you can do, but it may be worth seeking further advice based on your own circumstances.
∨ Yes ∨		
Have you lost your job because: you are pregnant; of your sex, race or disability; you refused to undertake dangerous or unsafe activities which posed a threat of physical injury; you tried to join a union; you 'blew the whistle' on wrongdoing at work; you asserted your right to be paid the Minimum Wage or took action against your employer for a breach of employment law?	>Yes>	You have probably been unfairly dismissed. You can take a case to an Employment Tribunal. It does not matter how long you have worked for your current employer — all dismissals on these grounds are automatically unfair (though employers will normally say that dismissal was for another reason).
∨ Yes ∨		
Have you worked for your employer for more than one year?	>No>	There may be nothing you can do. Unless your dismissal came about through one of the special cases above, your employer can dismiss you without saying why.

		However, you should look at your contract of employment. If this contains procedures such as notice periods or the promise of a formal hearing that were not followed then you may very well have a case. Seek advice.
∨ Yes ∨		
Does your employer say you are being made redundant?	>Yes>	You are only redundant if your job has ended, and no one is being taken on to do your job.
		Employers may select people for redundancy but they cannot discriminate on grounds of sex, race or disability.
		If there are any procedures for redundancy in your contract of employment then these must be followed.
		If there are more than 20 redundancies in a 90 day period then your employer must consult with the workforce. If there is a recognized union this must be with union representatives. If there is no union then special representatives must be elected. The consultation allows representatives to argue that the company should think again, to change the criteria by which people are selected for redundancy (say by increasing redundancy pay

or early retirement pensions and asking for volunteers) and/or to argue for more help such as training or job search for those who are to go.

Has your employer followed these procedures properly?

	˅ Yes ˅	˅ No ˅
	You are entitled to redundancy pay if you have worked for your employer for more than two years. The amount depends on your age, length of service and pay. Many employers will be more generous than these legal minimums: aged 18–21 – half a week's pay for each year of service; aged 22–40 – one week's pay for each year of service; aged 40–65 – one and half week's pay for each year of service.	You may have a case. Take advice.
	But weekly pay more than £240 is not counted and no more than 20 years' service can be taken into account.	

∨ No ∨		
Have you lost your job because: you cannot do it properly; of serious misconduct by you; of some legal requirement; you are over 65 and made to retire.	>Yes>	As long as your employer has followed proper procedures then you can be fairly dismissed for any of these reasons. However, if you have any doubts you should take advice. You may have a successful tribunal case if an employer has not got a fair system for judging conduct or capability. Any employee facing a disciplinary hearing can take a workmate or union official in with them. If this is denied then you may have a case. A tribunal may also disagree with an employer's judgement that your misconduct was serious enough to be punished by dismissal or that you could not do your job properly. If you are over 65 then your employer can force you to retire.
∨ No ∨		
If your employer cannot prove that you have been dismissed for one of these reasons then you have been unfairly dismissed.		

8 *Enforcing your rights*

Employers may deny you your legal rights for a number of reasons. They may simply not understand the law or fully appreciate their responsibilities as employers. While this is no excuse, there have been considerable changes in employment law since the 1997 election and it is perhaps not surprising that some employers have simply not kept up to date, or fully understood some of the finer points of complex provisions such as the Working Time Regulations. Once someone points out their legal obligations, however, they are unlikely to continue to deny you your rights.

Other employers know that they are breaking the law but hope they can get away with it. If challenged they too are likely to back down. Sometimes anonymous letters have allowed workforces to challenge this type of employer without having to identify a 'ringleader'.

In other cases your employer may genuinely believe he or she is acting correctly and within the law, but you, and your advisers, may disagree. Some of these cases illustrate where there is room for more than one point of view, such as whether your misconduct was serious enough to get you the sack. These cases are likely to end up in a tribunal, or be settled through one of the alternatives to a tribunal hearing described below. In other cases the law may not be clear, and a test case will be necessary to settle not just your case but that of many other people in your position.

One recent example of this process has been a series of court cases taken by Britain's trade unions that have established the rights of part-time workers to join company pension schemes. They established that companies that did not allow part-timers to join the pension scheme were breaking European sex discrimination law. This is because in most organizations the part-time workforce is mainly female, while full-time workers are more likely to be men.

The basic principle was relatively easy to establish, but how much compensation those who missed out on the chance to join good pension schemes should receive was less clear, as it depended on complicated legal arguments about how European law affected British law.

Because there is a lot of new employment law, and much of it began in Europe, there are likely to be further important test cases in the next few years. When the law uses words like 'reasonable' where there are value judgements involved, it usually takes one or more test cases to establish what the courts are likely to consider to be reasonable.

Many test cases involving large companies are not likely to cause bad feeling. No one would be surprised if a company, faced with a potentially big bill to compensate part-time staff who had not been allowed to join a pension scheme, tried to minimize the costs. Most companies would not take it out on the staff concerned.

But it is a different matter when you are taking on a company that deliberately exploits and bullies its staff. If it has sacked you then you have nothing to lose in taking action against it. But if you want to enforce your rights while still an employee you need to understand that even when the law is on your side, a vindictive company can still do a great deal to make your life miserable, particularly if you are acting on your own.

You do need to think through your options very carefully if you are in this position, and as we stress in so many parts of this book, you should take further advice. While the law is likely to be on your side (as soon as you take action to enforce your rights, you gain special protection against unfair dismissal, even if you have only just started working for your employer) there may be better ways to proceed, such as signing up fellow employees into a trade union and asking them to act on your behalf collectively so the employer cannot identify and victimize anyone. Some breaches of employment law can be investigated by external agencies such as the Health and Safety Executive, and you may want to call them in.

But if you do decide, after taking advice, that you need to take legal action then there are a number of different courts and tribunals that can hear claims relating to employment rights. Each has an appeal route if you or your employer wish to appeal against a decision. In the case of work-related welfare benefits, such as

Statutory Sick Pay, claims are dealt with by a separate system of tribunals (see Chapter 2).

Employment Tribunals and the courts

Bodies known as Employment Tribunals deal with most work-related legal action. Until 1998 these were known as Industrial Tribunals. Employment Tribunals operate in England, Wales and Scotland. In Northern Ireland the system is similar but the tribunals are called Fair Employment Tribunals and can also hear claims relating to religious discrimination, which is illegal in Northern Ireland.

These tribunals are specialist employment 'courts'. A tribunal will be made up of three people. The Chair will be legally qualified, and there will be two lay members, one of whom has been chosen as an employee representative and the other as an employer representative. As a panel, all members must exercise impartiality but the lay members will be expected to bring their employment experience to bear when judging the facts of the case. However, in some cases, the tribunal Chair will sit alone, particularly when there are any preliminary legal arguments. The tribunals are serviced by regional offices, which process the claims and arrange for the hearings.

Tribunals were originally intended to provide a relatively cheap, speedy and informal means of settling employment rights disputes between employees and employers. While they are still less formal than civil courts they have become more legalistic and formal as the law has become more complex.

However, most claims at tribunals are about unfair dismissal. Argument is therefore normally about the facts of the matter, rather than legal points, and you do not necessarily need legal representation – a union officer or advice worker may be better.

Civil courts

Not all employment-related cases go to a tribunal, and sometimes you can choose from a number of options. As we saw in Chapter 7 if you have been wrongfully dismissed – rather than unfairly dismissed – you can take a case either to a tribunal or pursue it through the civil courts. Civil courts, but not tribunals, can hear claims for breach of contract that do not involve dismissal, for example if your employer changes your contract without your agreement.

These courts can also hear claims for personal injury if you are injured in the workplace or suffer ill health as a result of your working environment and want to sue your employer for damages. For personal injury claims, you will need specialized legal help so we do not go into any detail here. Your union will probably have an arrangement with a firm of specialist lawyers and will pick up any legal costs. If you win, costs are likely to be awarded against the employer. If you are not in a union, then a local advice agency will be able to recommend solicitors who specialize in personal injury cases. Many solicitors will take such cases on a 'no win, no fee' basis if they think you have a good case.

A few employment-related matters might go to the criminal courts. For example, the Health and Safety Executive can prosecute employers who breach health and safety law. And if you do something illegal at work, such as stealing, or assaulting a colleague, you may be liable to criminal prosecution.

Where do I make my claim?

It is sometimes difficult to know *where* to pursue a claim. The rule of thumb is to check first to see whether the problem is covered by the list of issues dealt with by Employment Tribunals (see below).

You can make a claim at an Employment Tribunal under several 'heads'. For example, if your boss reduces your wages without your consent, and then sacks you without notice when you complain, on the grounds that you are black and he or she doesn't like black people, you can claim wrongful dismissal, race discrimination and unauthorized deduction from wages.

Some issues are not so easy to define. Common examples are stress and bullying at work (see Chapter 5). Sometimes these issues are directly related to another issue, which can be taken to a tribunal. Stress may be due to long hours, and working time issues can be taken to a tribunal. Bullying may include a sex discrimination aspect and this too can be taken to a tribunal.Often it will not be so simple. You can, however, sometimes rely on the 'implied' duty in your contract of employment for your employer to provide a healthy and safe working environment (see Chapter 5). For example, if you are constantly being picked on by an aggressive line manager for no obvious reason, and your complaints to more senior management have been ignored, then you can try and sue in either the County or High Court, depending on the level of compensation you wish to claim.

Such cases are often complex and you are advised to seek help. A trade union will have expertise in assessing your problem and looking for redress in the right place. If you are not a union member then you could take independent legal advice, perhaps from a law centre. However, if you are not eligible for Legal Aid, then you may face considerable legal costs.

You cannot pursue the same claim in two courts simultaneously, even where they both have jurisdiction on such matters. The term court here includes Employment Tribunals. Neither can you bring a claim again in another court after you have lost it in the first one.

Claims can now be heard against employers who are based outside the UK as long as you are ordinarily resident in the UK. If you are a citizen of another EU country, posted in the UK, you can now claim protection under UK law and submit a claim to an Employment Tribunal or court. Similarly, if you are a UK national working in an EU country you are covered by its employment protection and can make a claim in its courts.

It may be that you do not want to go to court or to an Employment Tribunal, in which case you could try and negotiate a settlement of the matter with your employer. This is covered in more detail later on in this chapter.

Cases dealt with by Employment Tribunals

These are the main areas of employment law dealt with by tribunals:

▌ equal pay;

▌ sex discrimination;

▌ race discrimination;

■ disability discrimination;

■ business transfers;

■ discrimination on the basis of trade union membership/non-membership, or activities;

■ time off rights for pension fund trustees, trade union and safety representatives;

■ wages issues, including National Minimum Wage and unlawful deductions;

■ wrongful dismissal (breach of contract);

■ unfair dismissal;

■ redundancy;

■ 'whistle-blowing';

■ working time and part-time working;

■ the right to be accompanied, or to accompany a colleague at a disciplinary or grievance hearing in the workplace;

■ the right to campaign for or against trade union recognition;

■ dismissal for taking lawful industrial action;

■ parental leave, maternity leave, leave for family emergencies;

■ dismissal for asserting a statutory right;

■ written statement of employment particulars;

■ written reasons for dismissal.

Making a claim

It is not difficult to make a claim to an Employment Tribunal. The first step is to fill out a form called an ET1. These are readily and freely available. You can get one from a Jobcentre, ACAS, your union, a local advice agency or the regional or national Employment Tribunal offices (see address section in Chapter 9). Although these forms are not difficult to fill in, it is very important to ensure that nothing which will help your case is left out and nothing which will damage your case is included!

Seek help from your trade union, or from a Citizens' Advice Bureau (CAB). While a CAB will give free assistance with filling out the form and general advice on your claim, they cannot represent you at the tribunal. Your union will normally be able to provide representation if it judges that your claim is likely to succeed. Once you have submitted the ET1 you will become known as the 'applicant'.

It is crucial that you stick to the time limits. For most cases, applications must be made within three calendar months of the 'effective date of termination' (usually the day on which you finish work) but there are some variations. See the timetable on page 26 for all the time limits. It is very hard to persuade a tribunal to accept a claim which is 'out of time', even if only by a day. It is worth using registered post so that you can prove when you posted the application, in case it arrives late because of postal difficulties beyond your control.

There is no legal aid available for representation at Employment Tribunals, although basic preliminary advice can sometimes be obtained under the Green Form scheme. This provides a short session with a solicitor to talk through any legal issue on a preliminary basis. Costs are very rarely awarded at tribunals, so you do not normally run the risk of having to pick up your employer's legal bill if you lose the case.

It is possible to represent yourself at a tribunal. The panel hearing the cases will try to help you. Although some people do successfully represent themselves, particularly in simpler cases, it is always best to try and have your own representative who is familiar with the way tribunals work. This is particularly important if your employer is going to be legally represented, and many automatically do this. You do not necessarily need to be legally represented. Union full-time officers are very experienced in taking cases to tribunals. If you are not in a union then you can consider employing your own solicitor, although as costs are rarely awarded at tribunals you will not normally be able to claim legal costs back from the other side if you win.

On the ET1 you will be asked to indicate the 'head' of claim. This means the category of jurisdiction into which the claim comes. This will be one from the list above, for example, unfair dismissal. You do not need to cite the legislation by its proper name, although if you can it does have the advantage of making the basis of your complaint absolutely clear to the tribunal.

You will also need to give details of the complaint and the remedy you are seeking. With any dismissal case you are advised to ask for reinstatement or reengagement. You are highly unlikely to get it – on average less than 1 per cent of claims result in reinstatement or reengagement – but it seems to have the effect of increasing the compensation, which you will probably get instead. It is also worth stating that you would like your claim to be heard by the full panel, as tribunals are increasingly trying to hear claims, at least at the preliminary stages, with the Chair sitting on his or her own. The advantage of the full panel is that there will be one member who has direct experience of your 'side' of the argument and you may get a more balanced judgement, at least on the facts.

You must be clear about whom the claim is against. If it is a discrimination claim, the employer will be sent a questionnaire (see Chapter 7). After receiving the ET1, the tribunal can ask you to give a written answer to a question if it thinks that this would provide helpful clarification. It is important to do this if it should ask, as it may help your case.

The ET1 has to be returned to the Central Office of the Employment Tribunals (the address is given on the form, and a helpful guidance booklet will be enclosed with the form). Your form and an ET2, which is a summons, are sent to the employer, who is known as the 'respondent'. Bear in mind that the employer will see everything you have written on your form, as will the tribunal panel, so be clear, be accurate and be polite! The employer then has to return an ET3 form, known as a 'notice of appearance', in which he or she will set out their defence.

Most employment rights are subject to eligibility requirements. The tribunal will first check that you are eligible to bring the case you have submitted. If you are not they will reject your claim. If there is any doubt then there will be a preliminary hearing, usually involving just the Chair.

For example to claim unfair dismissal, you must be an 'employee' in legal terms and normally have worked continuously for your employer for a year or more and you must send the form in within three calendar months of the 'effective date of termination' (normally your last day at work). If you do not meet any of these conditions then the tribunal will reject your claim. Each chapter of this book explains the eligibility requirements in each case and on page 26 there is a timetable showing the time limits for each type of claim.

When the ET3 is sent to the employer, a copy is sent to ACAS, who will offer you and the employer conciliation to try and settle the claim out of court. You are under no obligation to accept conciliation but assistance from ACAS, which is free, can be very useful at this stage. There is more about alternatives to tribunal hearings in Chapter 7.

If the tribunal decides that your case has no reasonable chance of success, it can hold a pre-hearing review, at which it may require you to pay a deposit of up to £150, which you will lose if you lose the case.

How tribunals work

There is a complex set of rules governing tribunal procedures and tribunals have considerable discretion in how to handle cases. You should provide as much supporting written evidence in advance of your hearing as possible. This is known as 'further and better particulars' in tribunal jargon. The tribunal can order both you and the employer to provide more evidence if it wants. It normally expects to see items such as written warnings, statements from witnesses, copies of the company disciplinary procedure, and pay statements. Either you or the employer may ask the tribunal to order disclosure of documents before the hearing if you feel that they are necessary to make a fair decision. The tribunal can also make witness orders, requiring witnesses for you or the employer to attend.

The tribunal will normally meet within three months from when you first submitted your ET1. It will tell you and your employer when the hearing is due. You or the employer can apply for a postponement if there is a genuine difficulty with the required time. Most tribunal hearings are held in large rooms, rather than formal court rooms. The three members of the panel will sit at the front, with the parties to the case and their representatives sitting opposite on the front row of chairs with others behind. Tribunal hearings are open to the public unless a specific request is made to the tribunal for a closed hearing and the tribunal agrees to this. This is normally only done in cases of great sensitivity, for example, involving sexual harassment, or where there are implications for national security.

Both parties will make an opening statement, presenting their case. Generally, the employer, or their representative, goes first but this depends on the nature of the case. An important consideration for the way the case proceeds is where the burden of proof lies. In some cases the onus is on you to show that your employer acted illegally. In others it is up to the employer to show they acted legally. For example, if you have been dismissed while you are pregnant, it is entirely up to the employer to show he or she had good reason to sack you. In other words the tribunal will assume you were dismissed unfairly unless your employer can prove that he or she sacked you fairly. In other cases (such as constructive dismissal) the burden of proof is with you, and you therefore have to prove your employer was in the wrong.

After the opening statements the tribunal will then go on to examine the parties, call their witnesses for cross-examination, examine the documentation, and finally call for closing statements from both parties. The tribunal can adjourn the hearing if time runs out or if either party wants to consider a settlement out of court at any time during the hearing. It can also stop proceedings if the respondent decides to concede the case, or if the tribunal decides that one party or the other is the clear winner and nothing would be gained by continuing the hearing. The panel will then decide whether you have won the case, and if so what compensation or other award you should receive. Each member of the three-person tribunal has an equal say, so it is possible for the lay members to outvote the Chair. However, panels generally try and reach a consensus. For straightforward cases, the decision will be given orally that day, with written confirmation and fuller reasons communicated in writing a few days later. A tribunal can delay making a decision in a more complex case.

Awards at Employment Tribunals

The tribunal can order reinstatement or reengagement but this is very rarely done in practice. Even when tribunals make such an order, employers commonly refuse to implement it. If your employer refuses to comply, you have to apply again to the tribunal. It will probably award you additional compensation in such a situation.

If your employer still refuses to comply, you have to pursue the matter in the County Court (Sheriff's Court in Scotland). Ultimately, your employer cannot be forced to take you back and the final penalty is compensation. If this cannot be recovered, you have to pursue the matter in the County Court. Unfortunately the costs of doing this often outweigh the benefit, although if your union is supporting you, the cost will be to the union rather than you.

Most often the tribunal will order compensation to be paid. A table showing the upper limits for compensation for the various types of claim is given on page 26. For discrimination claims, there is no upper limit and the compensation normally includes an element to cover hurt to feelings. For unfair dismissal the upper limit is £51,700. For wrongful dismissal claims in the tribunals, it is £25,000. These are upper limits however, and usually compensation awarded is well below these levels.

Compensation for unfair dismissal also includes an element to compensate for loss of earnings for the time between the dismissal and the tribunal decision. If you have got a new job, this element will be reduced to take account of what you are being paid. The compensation will also reflect other losses, such as loss of pension rights. There is an upper limit on the compensation for loss of earnings, which is uprated annually in line with the Retail Price Index. It is currently set at £240 a week. In some circumstances, employers can be made to pay more compensation if they failed to let you use an internal disciplinary procedure. Similarly, your compensation may be reduced if you refused to use one. The circumstances of employers are also considered, with smaller penalties for small businesses that are less likely to have formal procedures for dealing with workplace problems.

Appeals

If you lose the case, you can request the tribunal to review its own decision. You must do this at the hearing or within 14 days of the decision being recorded. The grounds for doing this are limited though. You would be likely to succeed, for example, if one of the parties was absent for part or all of the hearing, or if new evidence becomes available but not simply because you thought the decision was wrong.

Appeal is also possible to the Employment Appeal Tribunal (EAT) which sits in London for England, Cardiff for Wales and Edinburgh for Scotland. The EAT is a special appeal tribunal which only deals with employment-related issues, nearly all on appeal from the Employment Tribunals. The appeal has to be lodged within 42 days of the tribunal decision. A special form is required, which can be obtained from the Employment Tribunal office or directly from the EAT (see address at the back of the book). Appeals are only allowed on a point of law but this can include a 'perverse' decision by the tribunal where, for example, the members did not understand the facts. You will need a copy of the full written reasons for the tribunal's decision, which they will send you automatically and a copy of the Chair's notes, which you will have to request from the tribunal. It is possible to get legal aid for representation at the EAT and, as it will essentially be dealing with points of law, it is important to be properly represented by your union or by a solicitor. Unions may have in-house solicitors who will represent you, or may engage a solicitor for you and pay the costs. Your employer can also appeal.

Leave

Jackie Kuti was granted extended leave to visit her family in Nigeria. Before she went she signed a document headed 'contractual letter for the provision of holiday entitlement'. This letter made clear that Jackie agreed to return to work on 28 September. It said: 'If you fail to do this your contract of employment will automatically terminate on that date.'

When Jackie returned to England on 26 September she fell ill, and was unable to go back to work on the 28th. Her employers considered her employment had ended automatically according to the letter, and wrote to tell her so.

Jackie claimed unfair dismissal. She lost at both a tribunal and the Employment Appeal Tribunal. They ruled the letter was quite clear and that Jackie had breached her undertaking to return to work.

But the Court of Appeal disagreed. They ruled that Jackie had been asked to sign away her legal rights to be protected against unfair dismissal. But the law is clear that you cannot give up legal rights this way (with the exception of the right to redundancy payments if you are on a fixed term contract). Basically she had been asked to give up a right in return for an extended break.

This was an important test case. Following the judgement, employers cannot use 'automatic termination' clauses to get out of their duty to act reasonably in dismissal cases involving 'overstayers'. It is possible that similar 'automatic termination' clauses in other situations may also be found to be invalid on the same grounds.

Appeal from the EAT is to the Court of Appeal, but you need leave from the EAT to do this. Appeal from the Court of Appeal is to the House of Lords. You will certainly need legal representation at these stages.

It is also possible for a tribunal or any of the courts involved at an appeal stage to refer a case to the European Court of Justice. Only cases involving important legal principles that derive from EU law will go to Europe. It is likely to be a slow and expensive process, in which you will need the support of your union, or an organization such as the Equal Opportunities Commission.

It was not all right on the night

Jimmy Parker worked as a nightwatchman for his local council. He was sacked after being found absent from duty. He had signed the book as if he had worked a whole shift up to 7am, but was found home in bed.

Jimmy said he had gone home because he was ill, but he was dismissed on the grounds that he had absented himself from his security duties without permission and without informing his superiors or making an appropriate entry in the message/incident book. A general warning had been issued to all nightwatchmen a few weeks earlier to the effect that deliberate absence from duty would lead to dismissal. Jimmy had worked for the council for 27 years and had a previously good record of service. At a tribunal hearing Jimmy won a case of unfair dismissal on the grounds that given his age and record of service dismissal was an unduly harsh penalty. However, the Employment Appeal Tribunal reversed this decision. They said the council had acted reasonably because they had followed a fair procedure. Employees were aware of the consequences of such an action, and a proper appeals procedure had been exhausted.

As long as an employer follows a fair procedure it is up to the employer to decide whether or not to show leniency. It is not up to a tribunal to decide what they would have done in an employer's place. A clear message of cases like this is that as long as employers stick to a procedure that is more or less in line with the ACAS guidelines, then they are within their rights to dismiss you, as long as they apply the rules consistently, honour anything your contract of employment has to say about dismissal and do not discriminate.

Alternatives to tribunals and courts

There are various alternative ways of settling disputes with your employer that you should consider. Some of them will save you from having to pursue your claim in an Employment Tribunal or court.

You can reach a private agreement with your employer that they will pay you compensation, without necessarily admitting liability (indeed employers normally insist on this). An employer will also often require you to sign an agreement, which would have some legal force, saying that you will drop the claim in return for the agreed compensation payment. You are best advised to negotiate such a deal with the help of a lawyer or a union.

A wiser option is to ask ACAS to conciliate a formal agreement between you and the employer, known as a COT3. ACAS does not charge for its conciliation services. By doing this, you agree to accept a stated sum of money as compensation for the dismissal. Once you have signed this you will be barred from pursuing that claim any further. ACAS has a great deal of experience in these kind of cases, and can advise you on appropriate compensation amounts. This may be a particularly attractive option if you are not a union member and do not have the means to employ a solicitor to represent you at a hearing. A union may also advise you to go down this route.

A further option is to sign a 'compromise agreement', which is similar to a COT3 but need not involve ACAS. It must be signed by you and the employer and a person specified as having authority to sign compromise agreements according to the Employment Rights (Dispute Resolution) Act 1998. This will be a solicitor, a trade union officer or a CAB worker who has an appropriate certificate of indemnity insurance. Again, once you have signed a compromise agreement you cannot pursue that claim any further.

ACAS has recently established a new arbitration scheme for unfair dismissal claims. If you and your employer agree to go to arbitration, ACAS will appoint a qualified arbitrator, who will meet both of you in a formal hearing, probably, but not necessarily, in the workplace, hear both your arguments, listen to witnesses, look at relevant documents and then decide whether the dismissal was unfair. If the arbitrator decides that it was, he or she will order reinstatement, reengagement or compensation exactly as tribunals do.

This new scheme has real advantages. It is informal and quick, it is easier to represent yourself, it will look primarily at the facts of the matter without having to refer to case law, and it is much more likely to award reinstatement or reengagement than a tribunal. But there are also disadvantages. There is no right of appeal (although in exceptional circumstances judicial review may be available) and there are no lay members.

In general you should always take advice about which route is best for you in your particular circumstances. Your union or an advice agency, such as the Citizens' Advice Bureau, should be able to help.

Sources of advice and representation

You do not need to be a qualified lawyer to represent somebody at a tribunal. Indeed, it is wholly unnecessary to involve lawyers in many cases. Recently a number of independent advisers have started to advertise their services in local papers and by other means. They offer to prepare your case and represent you at a tribunal for a fee and/or a cut of your compensation.

You should be extremely wary of such advisers. While some may be competent, you have absolutely no guarantee that they have any expertise. The government is so concerned at just how badly some advisers serve their clients that they are currently considering whether they should be regulated. You should find out if their terms are reasonable. They may expect a very large share of any award you win. You should also discover their qualifications. Some claim that they have qualifications that they do not really have; others give themselves such names as 'legal advisers', which gives you the impression that they have some sort of legal qualification, when in reality this term means nothing.

The best representation you can have at an Employment Tribunal is probably a trained trade union representative. He or she will have considerable experience of how the tribunals work. They will also understand workplace issues and be able to spot errors made by your employer that an outside adviser would probably miss.

Surveys have consistently shown that in cases where the applicant is represented by a trade union, the applicant is more likely to be successful and will get much better compensation.

If you are not a member of a union, you may be able to get free legal advice from a local authority law centre if there is one near you. Most larger towns and cities have them. Otherwise, ACAS can provide advice, though not representation, as can staff at a Citizens' Advice Bureau. If you do want to use a solicitor, make sure you choose one who has direct experience of Employment Tribunal representation as solicitors often specialize in particular areas of the law. Someone who sold your house may have no experience of employment law.

9 *Further information*

In much of this book we have stressed the need to take further advice about your own particular circumstances if you have a problem at work. This chapter shows you where to find it.

Useful helplines and advice services

The TUC Know Your Rights Line
You can ring the TUC Know Your Rights Line on 0870 600 4 882. It can provide you with a series of up-to-date employment rights leaflets, which may add to the information provided in this book. It can also provide advice on an appropriate union for you to join. It is not staffed by trained advisers so cannot provide detailed advice.

The TUC Web site (www.tuc.org.uk) also contains employment rights advice and much up-to-date information about the world of work.

ACAS public enquiry points
ACAS, the Advisory Conciliation and Arbitration Service, is a publicly funded body that promotes good workplace relations. Its public enquiry points can provide advice on most of rights at work issues covered in this book. It helps both employees and employers. Phone the nearest one to you.

Birmingham	0121 456 5856
Bristol	0117 946 9500
Cardiff	01222 761126
Fleet	01252 811868
Glasgow	0141 204 2677
Leeds	0113 243 1371
Liverpool	0151 427 8881
London	020 7396 5100

Manchester	0161 228 3222
Newcastle	0191 261 2191
Nottingham	0115 969 3355

Or try the Web site www.acas.org.uk

The Employment Tribunal Service
If you need information about making a claim or tribunal proce-
dures you should call the Employment Tribunal Service Enquiry
Line on 0845 959775.

The Department of Trade and Industry
The DTI is responsible for many employee rights issues. It has produced short guides to a number of areas including new maternity
rights, parental leave and time off for dependants. The orderline is
0870 1502 100. The main Web site is www.dti.gov.uk

To go straight to employment rights material, contact www.dti.
gov.uk/er/index.htm

The **National Minimum Wage helpline** number is 0845 6000 678.
All complaints about underpayment of the National Minimum
Wage will be treated in strictest confidence (local call rates apply).

Alternatively you can write to them at: National Minimum
Wage Enquiries, FREEPOST PHQ 1, Newcastle-upon-Tyne NE98
1ZH.

Low pay units
West Midlands Low Pay Unit
Wolverley House
18 Digbeth
Birmingham B5 6BJ
Tel: 0121 633 4071
Local advice line: 0800 220 823

Yorkshire and Humberside Low Pay Unit
102 Commercial Street
Batley WF17 5DP
Tel: 01924 443850

Greater Manchester Low Pay Unit
23 New Mount Street
Manchester M4 4DE
Tel: 0161 953 4024

Scottish Low Pay Unit
24 Sandyford Place
Glasgow
G3 7NG
Tel: 0141 221 4491

Discrimination advice
There are three public agencies that provide advice respectively on
sex, race and disability discrimination. They not only provide
detailed advice but are also prepared to help present individual
cases:
Equal Opportunities Commission 0161 833 9244, www.eoc.org.uk
Commission for Racial Equality 020 7828 7022, www.cre.gov.uk
Disability Rights Commission 0845 622633, www.disability.gov.uk
LAGER (**Lesbian and Gay Employment Rights**) is a voluntary
body that can provide advice on 020 7704 8066 (women) 020 7704
6066 (men).
The Discrimination Law Association can provide information on
discrimination law and promotes access to representation for com-
plainants on 01933 225552, www.parish.oaktree.co.uk/dla/dla1.htm

Whistle-blowing
Public Concern at Work can provide advice on 020 7404 6609,
www.pcaw.demon.co.uk

Bullied at work
The Andrea Adams Trust
Maritime House
Basin Road North
Hove
East Sussex BN41 1WA
The Trust runs a confidential helpline on 01273 704900 which is
open from 10am–4pm Monday–Friday.

The Suzy Lamplugh Trust
14 East Sheen Avenue
London SW14 8AS
Tel: 020 8392 1839

Agency workers
The Department for Trade and Industry regulates employment agencies. It runs the Employment Agency Standards Line on 0645 555 105. This helpline takes up complaints against agencies from agency workers on matters including non-payment of wages and dangerous working conditions. Complaints to this line can result in prosecution of errant agencies and even their closure.

The Federation of Recruitment and Employment Services (FRES) on 020 7323 4300 is the trade association for employment agencies. It sets standards for its members. If the agency you are employed by has a FRES symbol on its premises or notepaper and you have a serious complaint about its behaviour, you can contact FRES who will investigate it on your behalf.

Health and safety
Health and Safety Executive information line on 0541 545500 can help with health and safety and working time issues. It has a wide range of free leaflets, not just dealing with specific hazards but also providing help and advice for groups such as homeworkers or pregnant women. Most can also be viewed at www.hse.gov.uk

Some issues are dealt with by the Environmental Health Department of your local council, including working time.

Working time
The Department of Trade and Industry's Workright number is 0845 6000 925. Use this to get copies of free government literature on the Working Time Directive. The Health and Safety Executive (see above) and the Environmental Health Department of your local council may be able to help and provide advice on your specific circumstances.

Family-friendly employment
Maternity Alliance – advice to pregnant women and new parents on 020 7588 8582.

Parents at Work on 020 7628 3565.
New Ways to Work (advice on flexible/'family-friendly' working patterns) on 020 7930 3355.

The law and advice agencies
The Law Society is the national body for solicitors. It does not provide legal advice, but can give you details of local solicitors that specialize in areas such as family law or personal injury. Its number is 020 7242 1222, www.lawsociety.org.uk

Law centres provide a free and independent professional legal service to people who live or work in their catchment areas. The Law Centres Federation will be able to tell you if you have a local law centre where you will be able to get free legal advice and possibly representation. Its number is 020 7387 8570 or try the Web site www.lcf.org.uk

The National Association of Citizens' Advice Bureaux can tell you about your local CAB on 020 7833 2181, or try the Web site www.nacab.org.uk. It also has Web pages at www.adviceguide. org.uk with advice on your rights, including employment rights.

Your local library will also be able to advise you of other local advice agencies that may be able to help.

Tax and Benefits
Inland Revenue (tax credits) 0800 597 5976, www.inlandrevenue. gov.uk
Benefits Agency (your local office will be in the phone book) www.dss.gov.uk

Criminal convictions
National Association for the Care and Resettlement of Offenders (NACRO) can provide help and advice for those with criminal convictions looking for work.
Tel: 020 7582 6500, www.narco.org.uk

Giving up smoking
ASH 0800 169 0 169, www.ash.org.uk

Drugs
The National Drugs Helpline is on 0800 776600

Alcohol
Drinkline is on 0800 917 82 82, www.alcoholconcern.org.uk

Britain's trade unions

If you want to join or contact a trade union, here is an alphabetical list together with the main occupations they cover. It can be confusing working out the most appropriate union to join. The TUC Know Your Rights Line can advise on which union or unions covers your job.

AEEU
Amalgamated Engineering and Electrical Union
Hayes Court, West Common Road
Bromley
Kent BR2 7AU
Tel: 020 8462 7755
www.aeeu.org.uk
Main trades and industries: manufacturing, engineering, energy, construction, IT, defence and aerospace, motor industry, civil air transport, chemicals and pharmaceuticals, steel and metals, shipbuilding.

AEP
Association of Educational Psychologists
26 The Avenue
Durham DH1 4ED
Tel: 0191 384 9512
e-mail: sao@aep.org.uk
www.aep.org.uk
Main trades and industries: educational psychologists in local educational authorities and other public and private organizations (England, Wales & Northern Ireland).

AFA
Association of Flight Attendants
AFA Council 07
United Airlines Cargo Centre
Shoreham Road East

Heathrow Airport
Hounslow
Middx TW6 3UA
Tel: 020 8276 6723
e-mail: 75452.2427@compuserve.com
e-mail: afa@afalhr.org.uk
www.afalhr.org.uk
Main trades and industries: airline cabin crew.

ALGUS
Alliance and Leicester Group Union of Staff
Croft House
Customer Services Centre
Narborough
Leicestershire LE9 5XX
Tel: 0116 200 3268/2259/2621
Main trades and industries: represents the majority of staff working for the Alliance and Leicester plc.

AMO
Association of Magisterial Officers
231 Vauxhall Bridge Rd
London SW1V 1EG
Tel: 020 7630 5455
e-mail: helen@amo.org.uk
Main trades and industries: magistrates' courts service in England and Wales.

AMU
Associated Metalworkers Union
92 Worsley Road North
Worsley
Manchester M28
Tel: 01204 793245

ANSA
The independent union for Abbey National Staff
2nd floor
16–17 High Street
Tring

Herts HP23 5AH
Tel: 01442 891122
e-mail: ansaoffice@compuserve.com

ASLEF
Associated Society of Locomotive Engineers and Firemen
9 Arkwright Road
London NW3 6AB
Tel: 020 7317 8600
Main trades and industries: railways (drivers, operational supervisors and staff).

ATL
Association of Teachers and Lecturers
7 Northumberland Street
London WC2N 5DA
Tel: 020 7930 6441
e-mail: info@atl.org.uk
www.atl.org.uk
Main trades and industries: teachers and lecturers in nursery, primary, secondary schools, sixth form and further education colleges.

AUT
Association of University Teachers
Egmont House
25–31 Tavistock Place
London WC1H 9UT
Tel: 020 7670 9700
e-mail: hq@aut.org.uk
www.aut.org.uk
Main trades and industries: academic and related staff in higher education.

BACM-TEAM
British Association of Colliery Management – Technical, Energy and Administrative Management
17 South Parade
Doncaster DN1 2DR

Tel: 01302 815551
e-mail: bacmteam@aol.com

BALPA
British Air Line Pilots Association
81 New Road
Harlington
Hayes
Middlesex UB3 5BG
Tel: 020 8476 4000
e-mail: balpa@balpa.org
www.balpa.org.uk
Main trades and industries: airline pilots and flight engineers
(commercial).

BDA
British Dietetic Association
5th Floor
Elizabeth House
22 Suffolk Street
Queensway
Birmingham B1 1LS
Tel: 0121 616 4900
e-mail: bda@dial.pipex.com
www.bda.uk.com
Main trades and industries: the science of dietetics in the private
and public sector.

BECTU
Broadcasting, Entertainment, Cinematography and Theatre Union
111 Wardour Street
London W1V 4AY
Tel: 020 7437 8506
e-mail: (general secretary) rbolton@bectu.org.uk
(admin officer) dcormack@bectu.org.uk
(press/publicity) jturner@bectu.org.uk
www.bectu.org.uk
Main trades and industries: broadcasting, film, video, theatre, cin-
ema and related sectors.

BFAWU
Bakers, Food and Allied Workers Union
Stanborough House
Great North Road
Stanborough
Welwyn Garden City
Herts AL8 7TA
Tel: 01707 260150
e-mail: bfawu@aol.com
Main trades and industries: food.

BOS
British Orthoptic Society
Tavistock House North
Tavistock Square
London WC1H 9HX
Tel: 020 7387 7992
e-mail: bos@orthoptics.org.uk
Main trades and industries: orthoptists.

BSU
Britannia Staff Union
Court Lodge
Leonard Street
Leek
Staffordshire ST 13 5JP
Tel: 01538 399627
e-mail: jaynebuxton@britanniasu.freeserve.co.uk
www.britanniasu.org.uk
Main trades and industries: finance sector union representing staff
working in Britannia Building Society and its group of companies.

CATU
Ceramic and Allied Trades Union
Hillcrest House
Garth Street
Hanley
Stoke-on-Trent ST1 2AB
Tel: 01782 272755

Main trades and industries: the ceramics industry (all areas).

CDNA
Community and District Nursing Association
Thames Valley University
32–38 Uxbridge Road
Ealing
London W5 2BS
Tel: 020 8280 5342
Tel: 0845 602 1281 (members advice line)
e-mail: cdna@tvu.ac.uk
www.cdna.tvu.ac.uk
Main trades and industries: community and district nurses.

Connect
The union for professionals in communications
30 St George's Road
Wimbledon
London SW19 4BD
Tel: 020 8971 6000
e-mail: union@connectuk.org
www.connectuk.org
Main trades and industries: telecommunications, information technology and related industries.

CSMTS
Card Setting Machine Tenters Society
48 Scar End Lane
Staincliffe
Dewsbury
West Yorkshire WF13 4NY
Tel: 01924 400206

CSP
Chartered Society of Physiotherapy
14 Bedford Row
London WC1R 4ED
Tel: 020 7306 6666
Main trades and industries: physiotherapy and health service.

CWU
Communication Workers Union
150 The Broadway
Wimbledon
London SW19 1RX
Tel: 020 8971 7200
www.cwu.org
Main trades and industries: posts and telecommunications in Post Office, British Telecom, Cable and Wireless, Cable TV, National Girobank and related technologies and industries.

CYWU
The Community and Youth Workers' Union
302 The Argent Centre
60 Frederick Street
Birmingham B1 3HS
Tel: 0121 244 3344
e-mail: cywuadmin@cywuhq3.freeserve.co.uk
Main trades and industries: youth workers, workers in youth theatre, community, community education, outdoor education, play.

EFTU
Engineering and Fastener Trade Union
42 Galton Road
Warley
West Midlands B67 5JU
Tel: 0121 429 2594

EIS
Educational Institute of Scotland
46 Moray Place
Edinburgh EH3 6BH
Tel: 0131 225 6244
e-mail: membership@eis.org.uk
www.eis.org.uk
Main trades and industries: teachers, lecturers, associated educational personnel (Scotland)

EMA
Engineers' and Managers' Association
Flaxman House
Gogmore Lane
Chertsey
Surrey KT16 9JS
Tel: 01932 577007
e-mail: hq@ema.org.uk
www.ema.org.uk
Main trades and industries: professional and allied staffs (managers, engineers and scientists) in aerospace, electricity supply, engineering, oil, shipbuilding and other industries.

EQUITY
British Actors Equity Association
Guild House
Upper St Martin's Lane
London WC2H 9EG
Tel: 020 7379 6000
e-mail: info@equity.org.uk
www.equity.org.uk
Main trades and industries: performance workers in theatre, film, television, radio and variety.

FBU
Fire Brigades Union
Bradley House
68 Coombe Road
Kingston-upon-Thames
Surrey KT2 7AE
Tel: 020 8541 1765
e-mail: office@fbu-ho.org.uk
Main trades and industries: local authority fire brigades.

FDA
Association of First Division Civil Servants
2 Caxton Street
London SW1H 0QH
Tel: 020 7343 1111

e-mail: head-office@fda.org.uk
www.fda.org.uk
Main trades and industries: civil service, public bodies and NHS.

GMB
22–24 Worple Road
London SW19 4DD
Tel: 020 8947 3131
e-mail: john.edmonds@gmb.org.uk
gmb.research@geo2.poptel.org.uk
gmb.information@geo2.poptel.org.uk
www.gmb.org.uk
Main trades and industries: civil air transport, security, AA, aerospace, defence, clothing, textiles, food production and distribution, retail, hotel, catering, chemicals and process, construction, building supplies, furniture and timber, local government, NHS, care, education, engineering, offshore, shipbuilding, energy, utilities.

GPMU
Graphical, Paper and Media Union
Keys House
63–67 Bromham Road
Bedford MK40 2AG
Tel: 01234 351521
e-mail: general@gpmu.org.uk
www.gpmu.org.uk
Main trades and industries: paper and board making, ink making, graphic design, graphic reproduction, printing, packaging, bookbinding and print finishing. National, regional and local newspapers. Clerical, administration and production workers in all areas of printing, publishing and allied trades, multimedia and information technology.

GSA
Guinness Staff Association
Sun Works Cottage
Park Royal Brewery
London NW10 7RR

Tel: 020 8963 5249
e-mail: elizabeth.jude@guinness.com
Main trades and industries: staff grades Guinness Limited,
Guinness Great Britain, Guinness Packaging, Guinness Northern
Ireland and Irish Bonding Group.

GULO
General Union of Loom Overlookers
9 Wellington Street
St John's
Blackburn BB1 8AF
Tel: 01254 51760
Main trades and industries: weaving manufacture.

HCSA
Hospital Consultants and Specialists Association
1 Kingsclere Road
Overton
Basingstoke
Hampshire RG25 3JA
Tel: 01256 771777
e-mail: conspec@hcsa.com
www.hcsa.com
Main trades and industries: hospital consultants, associate special-
ists, SoR grade and staff grade (all employed in the NHS).

IPMS
Institution of Professionals, Managers and Specialists
75–79 York Road
London SE1 7AQ
Tel: 020 7902 6600
e-mail: ipmshq@ipms.org.uk
www.ipms.org.uk
Main trades and industries: scientific, engineering, managerial
and professional staff in agriculture, aviation, defence, energy,
environment, health and safety, heritage, research councils.

ISTC
The Community Union
Swinton House
324 Gray's Inn Road
London WC1X 8DD
Tel: 020 7837 6691/2/3
e-mail: istc@istc-tu.org
www.istc-tu.org
Main trades and industries: all industries in and around steel and metal communities.

IUHS
Independent Union of Halifax Staff
Simmons House
46 Old Bath Road
Charvil
Reading
Berks RG10 9QR
Tel: 0118 934 1808
e-mail: 101670.3051@compuserve.com
Main trades and industries: all staff within Halifax plc, Halifax Financial Services Ltd, Halifax Independent Financial Advisers Ltd, Halifax Property Services, Halifax Direct, CMIG, Halifax Mortgage Services Ltd, LTS.

KFAT
National Union of Knitwear, Footwear and Apparel Trades
55 New Walk
Leicester LE1 7EB
Tel: 0116 255 6703
e-mail: headoffice@kfat.org.uk
www.kfat.org.uk
Main trades and industries: knitwear, lace, textiles, hosiery, dyeing and finishing, footwear, leather, gloving, made-up leather goods and other apparel.

MOMIMTS
Military and Orchestral Musical Instrument Makers Trade Society
2 Whitehouse Avenue

Boreham Wood
Hertfordshire WD6 1HD

MPO
Managerial and Professional Officers
Terminus House
The High, Harlow
Essex CM20 1TZ
Tel: 01279 434444
Main trades and industries: managers and professionals in the public sector: architecture and building services, education administration, engineering and allied professions, environmental health, finance, rating and central computing, general professional and management, health service, housing, legal and committee services, leisure services, libraries, museums, personnel and management services, planning, rent officers, scientific services, social services, supplies, trading standards, valuations and estates.

MSF
Manufacturing Science Finance
MSF Centre
33–37 Moreland Street
London EC1V 8HA
Tel: 020 7505 3000
www.msf.org.uk
Main trades and industries: 1. Engineers, craftspeople, scientists, technologists, professional and managerial staff in manufacturing industry (eg, aerospace and defence, engineering, automobiles, civil aviation, chemicals and pharmaceuticals, electronics and telecommunications, shipbuilding, tobacco, food and drink, energy, textiles, ceramics and paper). 2. Professional staff in universities, commercial sales, the voluntary sector, financial services and the National Health Service.

MU
Musicians' Union
60–62 Clapham Road
London SW9 0JJ
Tel: 020 7582 5566

e-mail: info@musiciansunion.org.uk
www.musiciansunion.org.uk
Main trades and industries: performers engaged in the music profession including music writers and instrumental music teachers.

NACODS
National Association of Colliery Overmen, Deputies and Shotfirers
19 Cadzow Street
Hamilton
Lanarkshire ML3 6EE
Tel: 01698 284981
Main trades and industries: mining.

NACO
National Association of Cooperative Officials
Coronation House
Arndale Centre
Manchester M4 2HW
Tel: 0161 834 6029
Main trades and industries: retail distribution, insurance, dairy industry, funeral services, motor trades (retail), retail pharmacy, travel industry, agriculture.

NAPO
National Association of Probation Officers
4 Chivalry Road
London SW11 1HT
Tel: 020 7223 4887
Main trades and industries: probation officers, including hostel assistant wardens and community service sessional supervisors.

NASUWT
National Association of Schoolmasters Union of Women Teachers
5 King Street
London WC2E 8HN
Tel: 020 7420 9670
e-mail: nigel.degruchy@nasuwt.org.uk
Main trades and industries: education.

NATFHE
The University & College Lecturers' Union
27 Britannia Street
London WC1X 9JP
Tel: 020 7837 3636
e-mail: hq@natfhe.org.uk
www.natfhe.org.uk
Main trades and industries: post school education, for example from GCSE to post-graduate studies – representing lecturers in prisons, adult education institutions, further education colleges, higher education colleges and universities.

NCTU
Northern Carpet Trades Union
22 Clare Road
Halifax HX1 2HX
Tel: 01422 360492
Main trades and industries: carpet industry and general section.

NGSU
Nationwide Group Staff Union
Middleton Farmhouse
37 Main Road
Middleton Cheney
Banbury, Oxfordshire OX17 2QT
Tel: 01295 710767

NUDAGO
National Union of Domestic Appliances and General Operatives
7–8 Imperial Buildings (first floor)
Corporation Street
Rotherham
South Yorkshire S60 1PB
Tel: 01709 382820
Main trades and industries: domestic appliance industries, engineering, foundries, electronics and general workers.

NUJ
National Union of Journalists
Acorn House
314–320 Gray's Inn Road
London WC1X 8DP
Tel: 020 7278 7916
e-mail: acorn.house@nuj.org.uk
Main trades and industries: journalists.

NULMW
National Union of Lock and Metal Workers
Bellamy House
Wilkes Street
Willenhall
West Midlands WV13 2BS
Tel: 01902 366651
Main trades and industries: lock and metal manufacturing industries.

NUMAST
National Union of Marine, Aviation and Shipping Transport Officers
Oceanair House
750–760 High Road
London E11 3BB
Tel: 020 8989 6677
Main trades and industries: Merchant Navy and all related areas.

NUM
National Union of Mineworkers
Miners' Offices
2 Huddersfield Rd
Barnsley
South Yorkshire S70 2LS
Tel: 01226 215555
Main trades and industries: coal mining.

NUT
National Union of Teachers
Hamilton House
Mabledon Place
London WC1H 9BD
Tel: 020 7388 6191
www.teachers.org.uk
Main trades and industries: teachers.

PCS
Public and Commercial Services Union
160 Falcon Road
London SW11 2LN
Tel: 020 7924 2727
www.pcs.org.uk
Main trades and industries: government departments and agencies, public bodies, private sector information technology and other service companies.

PFA
Professional Footballers Association
20 Oxford Court
Bishopsgate
Manchester M2 3WQ
Tel: 0161 236 0575
e-mail: info@thepfa.co.uk
www.thepfa.co.uk
Main trades and industries: professional football.

PLCWTWU
Power Loom Carpet Weavers and Textile Workers Union, includes the Generally Employed Members division
148 Hurcott Road
Kidderminster
Worcestershire DY10 2RL
Tel: 01562 823192
e-mail: gensec@carpetunion/gem.freeserve.co.uk
Main trades and industries: carpet industry.

POA
Prison Officers Association
Cronin House
245 Church Street
London N9 9HW
Tel: 020 8803 0255
Main trades and industries: persons employed in any penal or secure establishment or special hospital as a prison officer, a nursing grade, a non-industrial stores grade and special hospitals staff.

RMT
National Union of Rail, Maritime and Transport Workers
Unity House
205 Euston Road
London NW1 2BL
Tel: 020 7387 4771
e-mail: jknapp@rmt-hq.demon.co.uk
Main trades and industries: railways and shipping.

SCP
Society of Chiropodists and Podiatrists
53 Welbeck Street
London W1M 7HE
Tel: 020 7486 3381
e-mail: cs@scpod.org

SoR
Society of Radiographers
2 Carriage Row
183 Eversholt St
London NW1 1BU
Tel: 020 7391 4500
Main trades and industries: National Health Service.

SWSWU
Sheffield Wool Shear Workers Union
17 Galsworthy Road
Sheffield S5 8QX

T&G
Transport and General Workers' Union
Transport House
128 Theobald's Road
Holborn, London WC1X 8TN
Tel: 020 7611 2500
e-mail: tgwu@tgwu.org.uk
www.tgwu.org.uk
Main trades and industries: administrative, clerical, technical and supervisory; agriculture; building, construction and civil engineering; chemical, oil and rubber manufacture; civil air transport; docks and waterways; food, drink and tobacco; general workers; passenger services; power and engineering; public services; road transport commercial; textiles; vehicle building and automotive.

TSSA
Transport Salaried Staffs' Association
Walkden House
10 Melton Street
London NW1 2EJ
Tel: 020 7387 2101
e-mail: enquiries@tssa.org.uk
www.tssa.org.uk
Main trades and industries: administrative, clerical, supervisory, managerial, professional and technical, and research executive officers and allied employees of railways, road haulage, and road passenger undertakings. Also port authorities, waterways, hotels and catering, travel, shipping, railway rolling-stock manufacturers, and allied businesses in Great Britain and Ireland.

UBBS
The Union for Bradford and Bingley Staff
18d Market Place
Malton
North Yorkshire YO17 7LX
Tel: 01653 697634
Main trades and industries: all staff within the Bradford & Bingley Group.

UCAC
Undeb Cenedlaethol
Athrawon Cymru
Pen Roc
Rhodfa'r M(tm)r
Aberystwyth SY23 2AZ
Tel: 01970 615577
e-mail: swyddfa@ucac.cymru.org
Main trades and industries: education – teachers and lecturers.

UCATT
Union of Construction, Allied Trades and Technicians
UCATT House
177 Abbeville Road
London SW4 9RL
Tel: 020 7622 2442
e-mail: ucatt@psilink.co.uk
Main trades and industries: construction and building.

UNIFI
Sheffield House
1b Amity Grove
London SW20 0LG
Tel: 020 8946 9151
minicom 020 8944 5327

Churchill Court
Palmerston Road
Bournemouth
Dorset BH1 4HN
Tel: 01202 443600

Oathall House
Oathall Road
Haywards Heath
West Sussex RH16 3DG
Tel: 01444 458811
Www.unifi.org.uk

Main trades and industries: banking, insurance, building societies and financial institutions.

UNISON
UNISON Mabledon Place
1 Mabledon Place
London WC1H 9AJ
Tel: 020 7388 2366
www.unison.org.uk
Main trades and industries: local government, health care, the water, gas and electricity industries, further and higher education, transport, voluntary sector, housing associations.

USDAW
Union of Shop, Distributive and Allied Workers
Oakley
188 Wilmslow Road
Fallowfield
Manchester M14 6LJ
Tel: 0161 224 2804
www.poptel.org.uk/usdaw
Main trades and industries: retail, distributive, food processing and manufacturing, laundries, catering, chemical processing, pharmaceutical, football pools, home shopping, warehouses, insurance agents, clerical, milkround and dairy process.

UTW
Union of Textile Workers
Foxlowe
Market Place
Leek
Staffordshire ST13 6AD
Tel: 01538 382068
Main trades and industries: textiles.

WGGB
The Writers' Guild of Great Britain
430 Edgware Road
London W2 1EH

Tel: 020 7723 8074
e-mail: postie@wggb.demon.co.uk
www.writers.org.uk/guild
Main trades and industries: television, film, books, theatre and multimedia.

WISA
The Woolwich Independent Staff Association
40 High Street
Swanley
Kent BR8 8BQ
Tel: 01322 614957

Glossary

ACAS   The Advisory, Conciliation and Arbitration Service is a publicly funded agency that provides advice to both employers and employees on industrial relations issues. It offers guidance, conciliation, mediation and arbitration upon request where there is a dispute between a worker, or a union, and an employer. It produces helpful Codes of Guidance on issues such as disciplinary procedures.

accident book   A book that must be provided in every workplace by the employer, in which all workplace accidents must be recorded.

accredited training   Training which is recognized by an official training organization.

additional maternity leave   The 'extra' period of 29 weeks of unpaid maternity leave to which you are entitled on top of the 18 weeks of paid ordinary maternity leave if you have been continuously employed by the same employer for at least one year.

advances of wages   Some or all of your wages paid before you have done the work.

agency workers   Workers engaged through, or by, an employment agency or bureau and supplied to a hiring employer on a temporary basis. Some agencies employ their workers directly and should therefore provide their staff with a contract of employment. Other agencies contract workers to provide a service to the hiring employer. In this case you are probably self-employed, though possibly not for tax purposes, and will have a 'contract for service'.

annualized hours contract   A contract that specifies the normal number of hours to be worked over the period of a year (rather than a day, or a week). This kind of arrangement can be used in sectors where there are seasonal fluctuations, such as making ice cream or tourism.

antenatal care   Appointments at clinics or hospitals for pregnant women, relating to their pregnancy (an appointment with the doctor for an issue that is not directly related to the pregnancy, such as a sprained ankle, would not count as antenatal care).

applicant A worker who has submitted a claim to an Employment Tribunal or someone who has applied for a job.

apprentice A specific legal term describing a person contractually bound to an employer to learn a trade or profession.

assert a statutory right Ask an employer to give you something to which you are legally entitled; for example, a written statement of employment particulars.

back pay Wages or salary owed to you for work already performed.

bonuses Extra money for good performance, high productivity, etc.

breach of contract When either you or your employer breaks, or ignores the terms agreed in your contract of employment, either express or implied.

career break schemes Periods of leave, paid or unpaid, offered by an employer for employees to pursue other activities; usually only allowed after you have been employed by that employer for a set period of time.

casual worker A worker who is only employed when work is available, usually either on a temporary contract or on call when required to do a particular job or provide a service.

civil courts Courts that deal with non-criminal issues, for example, matrimonial issues, commercial disputes and employment law.

collective agreement An agreement between a trade union and an employer on behalf of a specified group of workers, usually relating to their pay and other working conditions.

comparator A legal term used in equal pay cases – another worker doing a job comparable to your own.

compromise agreement A legally binding agreement to accept compensation from an employer instead of pursuing a tribunal case; it must be signed by a solicitor, a designated trade union officer or a designated advice bureau worker.

constructive dismissal If you leave a job because conditions have become so bad that you cannot continue you could claim constructive dismissal in an Employment Tribunal, or civil court.

continuity of service Having worked for the same employer for a continuous period of time, ignoring breaks for maternity, sickness, holidays and some other temporary interruptions.

costs   When a court orders you to pay the legal costs incurred by the winning party, or when your costs are paid by the losing party.

COT3   A form used by ACAS when it conciliates an agreement between you and your employer that says you will accept compensation instead of making a claim at an Employment Tribunal.

crown servant   Some civil servants and government employees, who may have special terms and conditions of employment.

custom and practice   Something which has been done that way for a while. In particular, in employment law your contract of employment can change by custom and practice. For example, it may have become normal to allow staff to go home early on Christmas Eve and a court might decide that this has now been included in your contract of employment by custom and practice.

damages   Compensation when your employer causes you harm, either physical or in terms of your career prospects, injury to feelings, etc.

detriment   A legal term used to describe action taken by your employer against you unfairly, other than sacking you, such as refusing you training because you are in a trade union.

direct discrimination   A legal term meaning intentional discrimination, for example, saying that no women can apply for a driving job.

Directive   A piece of European Union law, many of which apply directly in the UK.

disciplinary hearing   A formal hearing organized by your employer where you are required to attend and answer for unsatisfactory performance of some sort.

disclosure of documents   A legal term used when an Employment Tribunal requires you or your employer to produce particular papers for the hearing, for example, timesheets.

dismiss/dismissal   Legal term for sack, or termination of your employment.

duty of care   Employers owe you a duty of care. This means that they are responsible for ensuring that you are cared for at work and do not have to work in unsafe or unhealthy conditions. This can include protection against bullying or stress. An implied duty of care exists in all contracts of employment.

effective date of termination   The date on which you finish working for an employer when you are dismissed or your contract expires.

employee   In law someone employed under a 'contract of employment', giving them a number of statutory and contractual rights.

employment status   The legal definition of whether you are a 'worker' or an 'employee' or 'self-employed'.

Employment Tribunals   Special courts of law which hear employment cases, for example, sex discrimination, unfair dismissal, non-payment of National Minimum Wage.

ET1   An application form on which you make a claim to an Employment Tribunal.

express terms   Terms that are specified in a contract of employment, for example, the amount you are to be paid.

final written warning   A final stage in a disciplinary procedure at work, after which you can be dismissed.

fixed term contract   A contract of employment that expires on a date specified in the contract.

full-time   There is no precise definition in UK law but generally considered to be working 35 hours a week or more.

further and better particulars   A legal term meaning documentation to be used in a tribunal hearing, for example, references, records of disciplinary hearings.

gross salary or wages   Wages inclusive of tax and National Insurance and any other elements, eg, performance-related pay.

guarantee payment   The minimum amount payable to you by your employer if you are laid off, or told to go home until work becomes available.

implied terms   Terms that are not written into your contract of employment but are considered to be part of it, for example, a duty to provide a healthy and safe working environment for you.

incapacity   Usually, medical reasons why you cannot work.

indirect discrimination   A legal term for discrimination which was not intended as such, for example, a requirement that you had to work until 10pm, which would indirectly discriminate against women, who are more likely to be the prime carers of children.

insolvency   When an employer is officially declared bankrupt.

itemized pay statement   A pay statement showing how your pay is made up. It will include terms such as basic pay, overtime, performance-related pay, gratuities and so on.

lay members   The non-legal 'side' members of an Employment Tribunal.

legal precedent   A ruling made in a court, which then influences future cases involving similar issues.

Maternity Allowance   Benefit paid to pregnant women/new mothers in some circumstances.

maternity certificate (MAT B1)   A certificate issued by your midwife confirming your pregnancy.

maternity leave   Time off work for pregnancy/childbirth.

National Minimum Wage   The least which you must be paid an hour.

notice of appearance   A document telling employers that they must respond to your application to have a claim heard by an Employment Tribunal.

notice of dismissal   A letter, or sometimes a verbal statement from your employer telling you that he or she intends to dismiss you on a certain date.

notice pay/payment in lieu of notice   You may agree to accept payment of wages for your notice period instead of continuing to work until your date of dismissal.

notified day of return   The date on which you tell your employer you will return after taking maternity or parental leave.

occupational pension   A pension scheme provided by your employer (as opposed to the state pension or any private pension you have); you may or may not have to contribute to your occupational pension.

on call   Available to work if required (typically social workers, security staff, etc).

ordinary maternity leave   The initial 18 weeks of paid maternity leave to which all employees are entitled.

out of time   Missing the deadline for submitting a complaint to an Employment Tribunal.

overtime   Hours worked over and above those specified in your contract.

parental leave   Unpaid leave for all parents of children under five born after 15 December 1999.

part-time   There is no legal definition but generally anyone working fewer hours than full-time staff.

passive smoking   Being exposed to other people's smoke.

perverse decision   A legal term meaning a decision which no normal or rational person would have made.

postponement   Legal term used when a tribunal puts off concluding a hearing, or starting a hearing until a future date.

pre-hearing review   Part of an Employment Tribunal procedure, when the Chair hears the basic details of a case and decides whether or not it is strong enough to proceed.

preliminary hearing   Part of an Employment Tribunal procedure in which the tribunal will decide a preliminary qualifying issue, for example, whether or not you are an 'employee' in the legal sense and can proceed with your case.

protective award   Where an Employment Tribunal makes a preliminary order to an employer not to do something such as making staff redundant, until it has had time to hear the case.

qualifying period   A legal term meaning the length of time you have been working for your employer in order to qualify for certain rights, for example, you must have worked for one year at least before you can claim unfair dismissal.

reasonable adjustments   Under the Disability Discrimination Act, an employer may be required to make certain adaptations to the working environment to allow a disabled worker to work for them, for example, installing a hearing loop facility.

recognize   The formal term for an agreement to negotiate certain workplace issues, for example, pay, or health and safety, with a trade union.

redundant/cy   When there is no longer the requirement for a job; the term redundant specifically applies to the job and not to the individual doing it.

reengagement   When an employee is allowed to go back to work after a dismissal to do the same or another job for that employer.

reference   Usually written but can be verbal, report by a past employer, or from a school or college, or a responsible impartial adult, about the abilities of a job applicant to do the job for which they are applying, or a statement about how they did their previous job.

reinstatement   When you are restored to your previous job after a dismissal.

resigned   When you leave your job.

respondent   The employer against whom a claim is being made at an Employment Tribunal.

retired   No longer working, usually due to age but sometimes illness.

RSI   Repetitive Strain Injury; an injury or condition caused by doing the same thing over and over again at work, eg, word processing.

self-certification form   When you take time off sick, for the first period you write a letter to your employer saying that you were off for whatever reason.

self-employed   Not contractually bound to an employer as 'an employee' though you may be contracted to provide a service to them; usually paying your tax and National Insurance yourself.

severance payment   This is not a precise legal term in the UK. Normally it refers to a payment made to you by an employer in return for you agreeing to leave without pursuing a claim against your employer.

sexual orientation   Your sexuality.

split shifts   Working part of a shift, then taking time off, then resuming work. An example might be working in a pub or restaurant for four hours over lunch-time and then working another four hours in the evening.

staff handbook   Explains how the company operates, its aims and objectives, and, usually, general terms and conditions of employment. It may be given to you when you start work and all or part is likely to be a legal document if it sets out some of your terms and conditions.

Statutory Maternity Pay   The minimum which you must be paid during your 18 weeks of ordinary maternity leave.

Statutory Sick Pay   The minimum you must be paid when you are off sick.

suspension   When you are sent home from work, usually during a disciplinary procedure, often on full pay, pending a decision being made on whether or not to dismiss you.

temporary workers   Those engaged for a short time, or to do a particular job.

terms of your contract   What your contract says about your conditions of work; terms are legally binding on you and your employer once you have started working under them and by doing so you have agreed to them.

transfers of undertakings   When a business changes owners, typically from the public to the private sector.

unauthorized deduction from wages   Money taken out of your wages without your permission and without it saying in your contract that it may be done.

unfair dismissal   Legal term for a dismissal carried out for no good reason or without going through an agreed company procedure for dismissals.

verbal warning   Usually part of a disciplinary procedure, a first warning, to be followed by a further warning, probably written, if you do not improve your performance, or stop doing something wrong.

visual display units (VDUs)   Computer screens.

void   Legal term meaning a term in a contract that is not valid, for example, if your contract states that you will be paid less than the National Minimum Wage.

waive   a legal term meaning to agree to do without something, eg, agreeing that you will not get Statutory Redundancy Pay if you are on a fixed term contract lasting more than two years.

whistle-blowers   Making a complaint outside the organization for which you work about malpractice in the workplace. In some circumstances you are legally protected against detrimental action by your employer as a result.

witness orders   A legal term meaning an order in a court or tribunal to require a witness in a case to attend court or produce a statement.

worker   A legal term that goes wider than employee. The difference is that an employee either has, or is entitled to, a contract of employment. Someone who is a worker but not an employee works for someone else but usually on the basis of providing a service. Strictly speaking all employees are workers, but not all workers are employees. In practice however, worker is often used to describe those who are not employees.

written statement of employment particulars   A legal document, not, strictly speaking a contract, in which your basic terms and conditions of employment are set out. However your contract of employment may include your written statement.

written statement of reasons for dismissal   A legal term for a letter from your employer stating why you have been dismissed.

written warning   Usually the middle or final part of a disciplinary procedure, in which you are told that if you do not improve you will be disciplined or dismissed.

wrongful dismissal   A legal term meaning that your employment has been terminated in a way that does not follow the procedures in, or in some other way goes against, your contract of employment. A common example is not getting enough notice.

zero hours contract   A contract of employment which is legally binding on you, so that you are obliged to work when asked to, but which does not specify your hours and states that when you are not required to work you will not be paid.

Index

Index of advertisers